Judgment and Decision in Public Policy Formation

AAAS Selected Symposia Series

Published by Westview Press
5500 Central Avenue, Boulder, Colorado

for the

American Association for the Advancement of Science
1776 Massachusetts Ave., N.W., Washington, D.C.

Judgment and Decision in Public Policy Formation

Edited by Kenneth R. Hammond

AAAS Selected Symposium 1

AAAS Selected Symposia Series

Published in 1978 in the United States of America by

Westview Press, Inc.
5500 Central Avenue
Boulder, Colorado 80301
Frederick A. Praeger, Publisher and Editorial Director

Library of Congress Number: 77-90417
ISBN: 0-89158-428-5

Printed and bound in the United States of America

About the Book

From various vantage points the authors consider the topic of judgment and decision in policy formation. Richard Lamm, governor of Colorado, describes the problem of utilizing scientific knowledge in the context of political survival. Joseph Coates, assistant to the director, Congressional Office of Technology Assessment, explores the nature of public policy issues. Kenneth Hammond, director of the Center for the Study of Judgment and Decision in Policy Formation at the University of Colorado, describes the competence of thought that can be brought to bear on public policy issues. Paul Slovic, Decision Research Inc., addresses the problem of risk assessment in policy formation from the point of view of a cognitive psychologist. Ward Edwards, director, Social Science Research Institute, University of Southern California, describes the general manner in which decision theory may be applied to policy formation. Kenneth Boulding, program director, Institute of Behavioral Science, University of Colorado, provides an overview of judgment and decision in policy formation. Hillel Einhorn, professor of industrial psychology, University of Chicago, shows the consequences of fallible judgment for social policy formation. Kenneth Hammond and Leonard Adelman provide an example of the application of judgment analysis to a public policy issue.

Contents

List of Figures

List of Tables

Foreword

The *AAAS Selected Symposia Series* was begun in 1977 to
provide a means for more permanently recording and more
widely disseminating some of the valuable material which is
discussed at the AAAS Annual National Meetings. The volumes
in this *Series* are based on symposia held at the Meetings
which address topics of current and continuing significance,
both within and among the sciences, and in the areas in which
science and technology impact on public policy. The *Series*
format is designed to provide for rapid dissemination of information, so the papers are not typeset but are reproduced
directly from the camera copy submitted by the authors, without copy editing. The papers are reviewed and edited by
the symposia organizers who then become the editors of the
various volumes. Most papers published in this *Series* are
original contributions which have not been previously published, although in some cases additional papers from other
sources have been added by an editor to provide a more comprehensive view of a particular topic. Symposia may be reports of new research or reviews of established work, particularly work of an interdisciplinary nature, since the AAAS
Annual Meeting typically embraces the full range of the
sciences and their societal implications.

WILLIAM D. CAREY
Executive Officer
American Association for
the Advancement of Science

About the Editor and Authors

Kenneth R. Hammond is the director of the Program of Research on Human Judgment and Social Interaction, Institute of Behavior Science, and professor of psychology at the University of Colorado, Boulder. He studied under Egon Brunswick and has contributed to the theoretical framework and the empirical foundations of Brunswick's probabilistic functionalism. Hammond's recent research includes studies of interpersonal conflict which arises from differing cognitive systems and studies of interpersonal learning. He has published widely, most recently coediting Psychoactive Drugs and Social Judgment: Theory and Research *(Wiley, 1975).*

Leonard Adelman is acting director of the Center for the Study of Judgment and Decision in Policy Formation, Institute of Behavioral Science, University of Colorado. He is also a consultant to the State of Colorado and has published in the areas of policy formation, social judgment theory, group psychology, and technology assessment.

Kenneth E. Boulding is professor of economics at the University of Colorado, Boulder, and director of the Program of Research on General Social and Economic Dynamics, Institute of Behavioral Science at the University. He has taught, lectured and published widely and is the recipient of many honorary degrees. He is a Distinguished Fellow of the American Economic Association and a member of the National Academy of Sciences. Boulding's most recent book is The Social System of the Planet Earth *(Addison-Wesley, 1977).*

Joseph F. Coates is Assistant to the Director of the Office of Technology Assessment of the U.S. Congress and is former program manager for technology assessment at the National Science Foundation. His major interest is planning for the future, with primary emphasis on the impact of technology on society. He has published numerous papers dealing with public affairs, technology assessment, military affairs, and criminal justice.

Ward Edwards is a research psychologist and professor in industrial and organizational psychology and is director of the Social Science Research Institute at the University of Southern California. He has published widely on investigations of subjective probability preferences, statistical decision functions, behavioral decision theory and modeling the psychological aspects of human decision-making.

Hillel J. Einhorn, professor of behavioral science at the Graduate School of Business, University of Chicago, specializes in research methodology, statistical methods in the behavioral sciences, and models of human judgment and decision-making. He has published numerous articles and is on the editorial board of Organizational Behavior and Human Performance.

Richard D. Lamm, governor of Colorado since 1975, is an attorney and a former member of the Colorado House of Representatives. He has been an associate professor of law at the University of Denver, and is concerned with law and public policy.

Paul Slovic is a research associate with Decision Research in Eugene, Oregon, and adjunct professor of psychology at the University of Oregon. He is the author of numerous articles in the areas of judgment, decision processes, and risk taking, and is on the editorial boards of several journals. Slovic is also currently a consultant to the Food and Drug Administration.

Introduction

    This book brings together the thoughts of a practicing
politician (Richard Lamm, Governor of the State of Colorado), a scientist in government (Joseph Coates, Assistant
to the Director of the Congressional Office of Technology Assessment), several researchers in the field of
judgment and decision analysis (Leonard Adelman, Ward
Edwards, Hillel Einhorn, Kenneth Hammond and Paul Slovic),
and those of an outstanding and well-known economist
(Kenneth Boulding).

    The chapters that constitute the core of the book
are those by Boulding, Coates, Edwards, Hammond and Slovic.
These chapters are somewhat expanded versions of the
papers they read at a symposium entitled "Judgment and
Choice in Public Policy Formation" held in Denver, Colorado,
at the 1977 meetings of the American Association for the
Advancement of Science. The symposium was intended to
bring to the audience the views of a scientist in government (Coates) who is not only conversant with
the problem of public policy formation, but is actively
engaged in that process, particularly as it is involved
with the choice of whether and how, to make use of modern
technology in the public interest. The symposium was
also intended to set alongside Coates' remarks the views
of three researchers in the field of judgment and decision,
so that the audience might observe the nature of that work
and to what extent it bears upon public policy formation
as described by Coates. And, finally, the symposium was
also intended to provide the audience with the reaction
of an economist long concerned with public policy to the
remarks of the other panelists. And that is what is
included in this book.

Three additional papers are included, however, because of the special contribution they make to this topic. As the chief executive of the state that hosted the meetings Governor Lamm delivered a major address to the members of the AAAS at the meetings. And because that address bears directly on the issues considered in the symposium, and because Governor Lamm, as a practicing policy maker brings a perspective to this topic that none of the other speakers do, his speech is included as the first chapter in the book. Readers will do well to consider carefully Governor Lamm's comments about the relation (or non-relation) between scientists and politicians.

A second paper was added to the symposium papers because it provides an excellent example of the sort of analysis a judgment and decision researcher brings to a problem that plagues modern society--welfare payments. Hillel Einhorn shows how an analytical treatment of that problem leads to an entirely different perspective than one gains from the ordinary policy analysis--or the syndicated news columnists.

Finally, a third paper was added, also in the interests of providing an example of the use of judgment and decision analysis in public policy formation. In this example, Hammond and Adelman show how scientific information can be integrated with the social values of policy makers and the public in order to produce a rational approach to a problem that divided a city into apparently irreconcilable factions.

Having told the readers what they might find here, a word should be said about what they will not find. They will not find a thoroughly integrated set of papers that direct themselves to a narrow topic. The authors remarks range over a number of issues, often in an idiosyncratic way. Governor Lamm's surprise at not having made large use of the scientific talent available to him is partly explained by Coates' acerbic and unflattering remarks about the egocentric behavior of academicians. But this topic was not discussed by the other speakers. Nor did Boulding speak directly to all the problems discussed by the researchers in judgment and decision analysis. No one will want to miss the satire in the poem that he wrote while listening to the papers that went before him, however.

In short, what the reader will find are the present views of persons who are not only concerned with improving the quality of judgment and decision in public policy formation, but are trying to do something about it.

Since one of the purposes of the symposium was to
stimulate people to develop an interest in this topic, on
the last page of the book we include a short list of
articles and books that will prove useful in this regard.

The Environment
and Public Policy

Richard D. Lamm

I am honored to appear before the American Association
for the Advancement of Science today. I have no scientific
credentials, and few political ones, so I will speak only
as a public policy maker who worries a lot. Serving the
public is an increasingly hazardous duty--but I believe
public policy to be one of the greatest challenges of our
time.

It is my deep belief that we are faced with a crisis
of crises--and that our political and scientific solutions
are not keeping up with the pace of problems. Further I believe that we truly live in a hinge of history--and that we
will see dramatic change in the years ahead. Some of this
change will be helpful--some harmful--but on balance I believe that the crises we are faced with are moving us into
the most hazardous time of human history. We are sailing
speedily into a world as new and unknown as the world Colum-
bus sailed into, and neither the politicians nor the scientific community are prepared for the nature and extent of
change.

None of the problems are new to you--thermonuclear destruction, the energy crisis, lack of confidence in our
institutions, the population explosion, pollution and deple-
tion of natural resources, and many more. In each of these
areas, I believe that the solutions are lagging far behind
the problems. We are entering into a watershed time of
human history with serious flaws in our problem solving
machinery. Neither our institutions nor our value systems
are structured to meet the challenges of our times. Because
of this, problems which could be solved in a timely manner
are not being solved, or in many cases not even worked on.

It is clear that the public today looks to both scientists and politicians to help them out of the Niagara of problems which are coming at them. They have a great faith in science and technology, and, despite Watergate, a high hope for a political leader who can lead them to a better life. As a recent pollster stated, they have "high hopes but low expectations" that we will produce an effective political leader who will help us solve the coming problems of energy crisis, drought, inflation, unemployment, and natural resource consumption.

The truth is, however, that we have very little leadership in politics any more; we now have umpires. Politicians survive because they don't rock boats, because they are usually chosen in a game which makes the common denominator the most likely winner.

Science is a process which seeks truth--politics is a process which seeks <u>survival</u>. Survivability is that quality which makes in the political value system a successful "politician." We can lament this fact, criticize it roundly, pray for "profiles in courage" but inevitably we are surely to live our future, as we have observed in our history, with "survivability" as an overriding consideration in virtually every political judgment.

Where the scientist will put forth his findings, and conclusions and ask for criticism so that the "feedback loop" is complete--a politician stays as far away from criticism as he or she possibly can. Kenneth Boulding has described the differences well in an article in <u>Science</u>:

> The relationship between the scientific and the political communities is one of constant mutual frustration. There is a feeling on both sides that each ought to be able to help the other. The political community is constantly faced with making what it thinks are at least important decisions. Every decision involves the selection among an agenda of alternative images of the future, a selection that is guided by some system of values. The values are traditionally supposed to be the cherished preserve of the political decision-maker, but the agenda, which involves fact or at least a projection into the future of what are presumably factual systems, should be very much in the domain of science. Bad agendas make it much harder to make good decisions and if the decision-maker simply does not know what the results of alternative

actions will be, it is difficult to evaluate unknown results. The decision-maker wants to know what are the choices from which he must choose. It is not surprising, therefore, that there is a demand for a one armed scientist or economist without that infuriating other hand.

The culture of the political community is very different. It is dominated in the first place by lawyers who are trained to win cases rather than to solve problems. The lawyers' "problem" is not to produce testable propositions, but to win the case. For politicians, likewise, the problem is to win elections and to please the majority of their constituents. The "scientific" problem-solving which is involved in getting the best legislation of the best decisions is incidental to the larger problem of political survival. We should not necessarily blame lawyers and politicians for behaving like lawyers and politicians. It is, in fact, what we hire them and elect them to do. The legal and political subculture is not the result of pure chicanery and foolishness. It has evolved over many generations for some very good reasons. The main reason is that where decisions involve distributional changes, that is, where they make some people better off and some people worse off, problem-solving in the scientific sense would not come up with any answers. Legal and political procedures, such as trials and elections, are essentially social rituals designed to minimize the costs of conflict. The price of cheap conflict, however, may be bad problem-solving in terms of the actual consequences of decisions. So far, the social invention that will resolve this dilemma does not yet seem to have been made. [But see chapters 2, 3, & 4, this volume: Ed.]

The policy maker in elective office is constantly faced with a classical dilemma--he sees the need for dynamic new policies but questions his political survivability if he proposes them. Whatever pretensions of courage he claims, he is caught between what he knows to be necessary and what he thinks will be accepted politically. Every critical decision may be his last. The raven sits on his shoulder and for every decision whispers "evermore." The dilemma is historic and has been faced by political figures throughout history. Al Smith, one of the world's most practical politicians, once said "A politician can't be so far ahead of the band he can't hear the music." His value

system placed political survivability at the absolute top
of his priorities, and however "progressive" his thinking
it was within the relatively continuing context of the next
election.

Why do we want to survive? For many simply complicated,
idealistically selfish reasons.

In Colorado and most states it is not to feather our
nests; there is stupidity in the legislative process, but
little actual corruption. The reason is not that simple.
For one thing the petty fame attached to the smallest, least
prestigious office is itself corrupting. Most of our legislators can't be called Dr. or Professor or Esquire.

Once in a while someone with Old Testament eyes stum-
bles into the process and wants to change things in ways
that do not accord with the rules, but he is soon neutral-
ized. Most of us find in the words of one of the most
successful people in my profession, The Honorable Everett
Dirksen, that the oil can is mightier than the sword.

We also want to survive because though we are bit actors, it's still the most exciting show around. There is a
tension, an excitement, an illusion of power if not actual
power. We want to survive to be there.

As John F. Kennedy said: "Winning isn't everying--but
losing, that's nothing." We do not have tenure--we want to
survive.

It is highly likely that within a democratic framework
the focus on survival will continue to hold. Ideally, perhaps, one can long for heroic political figures who are
willing to take a long lead off the safe second base of
political respectability. However, even when one does
find his own profile of courage he is seldom in a position
to succeed in passing legislation alone. Democracy is advanced by a heroic legislator, but legislation ultimately
only succeeds by a full majority of conventional politicians.
We live with myopia--as one Speaker of the U.S. House of
Representatives stated "What do I care about posterity--
what has it every done for me?".

Let me now evaluate how a policy maker--or at least
this policy maker evaluates the contributions and the
failings of the science and technology community. I am a
little taken aback when I think of why I, as a Governor of a

state with a myriad of problems, don't use more of the
scientific resources I have here in this state. Most of
the fault is mine, but not all. I find that the scientific
community has a tendency to formulate problems narrowly--to
have a specialized tunnel vision which does not see or fully
appreciate all the public policy factors of a decision.
Biologists use biological modes, economists use econometric
models, engineers mechanical models. Comprehensive policy
is not readily adapted to such modes. (See also chapter 2:
Ed.)

In addition to finding too often single dimensional
solutions to multifaceted problems it would appear to this
decision maker that scientists often tend to ignore resource limitations and the agony of politically implementing
many of the proposed "solutions." We speak to each other
across our "two cultures" but we seldom communicate.
Universities are looked at more as budget problems than as
exciting resources to be used. As Coates points out in
chapter 2, this state of affairs is not solely the fault of
public officials.

Public policy--diamond like--takes on a new dimension
every direction it takes. We need more than bright minds,
we need wisdom. But science at best is not wisdom, it is
knowledge, while wisdom is knowledge tempered with judgment.
This judgment is too often missing in the accelerating pace
of scientific advance. Lewis Mumford, writing on the auto-
mation of knowledge, states it succinctly: ". . . decisions
of critical importance to the human race are being taken
today on the basis of ten year old knowledge, confidently
applied by highly disciplined specialists who too often
display the short comings of ten year old minds, for they
regard as a special merit their deliberate practice of
cutting their minds off from ten thousand years of human
experience and culture. . . strangely, they have not even
a suspicion that the vast quantity of exact knowledge now at
our dispoal is no guarantee whatever of our having sufficient emotional sensitiveness and moral insight to make
good use of it; if anything, the contrary has already proved
true." (See chapter 3 for a discussion of the role of judgment in public policy formation.)

I find that one of the great challenges of the future
will be to differentiate what science and technology can
do from what it cannot do. Its promise is great--it can
and will continue to make dramatic breakthroughs in field
after field--it can continue to improve significantly the

human condition--but as a policy maker, I fear that people have too much faith in its miracles, that the cornucopia of its benefits can seriously excuse, postpone and delay some public policy considerations which we must institute.

Science and technology are seen as the twentieth century equivalent of the miracle of the loaves and fishes--a solution to not only some of our problems--but to all of our problems. Farming the sea is unlikely to "solve" the problem of a population exploding dramatically in a world which hardly affords sufficient diet to 50 per cent of its inhabitants. Miracle grains are impressive, but we increasingly are doubtful if we can sustain the investment in energy, water and capital to have that be a long lived solution.

We need badly in most parts of the world an ethic which makes people want fewer kids--more than the perfect contraceptive. We need social innovation as badly as we need scientific innovation. We rely on only technological solutions at our hazard.

We live in the midst of a large intellectual schizophrenia. One world view held by many very good and intelligent people is that our current economic problems are merely temporary hiccups in the system that will soon give way to Daniel Bell's salubrious vision of the "post-industrial state." This vision of American forecasts shorter workweeks, abundance for all, and a constantly rising per capita income. The economic pie will continue to grow, says this scenario, indeterminately. The other vision of America is that we are heading into an age of scarcity. There are "limits to economic growth," goes the argument, which require us to make new institutional arrangements.

It is axiomatic that our definitions of our problems control and dictate how we define the solutions. If shortages of energy or of natural resources are caused by inadequate supply, the solution is simple: increase supply. If, however, the shortage is due to excessive demand, the solution is vastly different. In fact, it urges us to invest our time, capital, and efforts in almost the opposite direction. Is our economic glass half-empty or half-full? Are shortages caused by inadequate supply or excessive demand? It is, alas, more than just a difference of opinion. It becomes a major public policy decision. As one source put it recently in an editorial on the energy crisis:

Had the United States moved soon enough, much could
have been done to avert the crisis. Mass transit
could have been encouraged over highway building,
bringing great savings in fuel as well as comfort.
Research into ways to remove pollutants from coal or
to turn it into gas or oil could have been pushed
harder; that would have enabled the country to make
greater use of the abundant fuel. Building codes
could have been changed to require more effective
heat-conserving insulation of homes.

Instead, with remarkable consistency and perverse
ingenuity, the nation kept doing exactly the opposite
of what was required. For almost two decades,
Washington has been spending tens of billions of dollars to subsidize highway building. Almost every
American office building has been constructed with
closed air systems that require air conditioning no
matter what the outside temperature.

We have a limited supply of capital and capital formation potential. Impressive as our economic might is, it
has very definite limits. Capital--others have stated so
well--is our stored flexibility to adjust to tomorrow's
problems. How we invest that capital is a public policy
decision which well might dictate whether or not our social, political and economic system survives the bumps and
shocks ahead. Do we "develop" our way out of shortages by
synthetic fuels, massive federal programs like Vice President Rockefeller proposed of spending $100 billion--or do
we "conserve" our way out of them? Do we attempt to feed
the voracious consumption we have accustomed ourselves to,
or do we put it on a diet? We probably have to do some of
both--both develop and conserve-- but these are not equal
on the national agenda nor in our cultural heritage.

Our whole intellectual and social history urges a
clear way out of shortages--a formula of drill, mine and
refine, a strategy that is pushed by our belief in the infinite and of boundless frontiers, limitless resources and
a total belief in science.

We move to solve today's problems as we have solved
so many others: roll up our sleeves, use our American
ingenuity, call upon our puritan heritage, push aside the
doubters, and get to work. However, history has a way of
playing tricks on civilizations. "New occasions teach new
duties, time makes ancient good uncouth" says the old

Presbyterian hymn. History is made by men and women who
recognize that civilizations are changed by people who
think Copernican thoughts.

I do not believe that the transportation crisis will
be solved by more super highways or faster airplanes--nor
our energy use curbed by working on the supply side of the
equation--as opposed to the demand side. Nor do I believe
we can live sane lifestyles by Keynesian solutions which
pump the economy into new and more magnificent excesses of
consumption. It is not necessarily physical limits to
growth--nor resources--but a realistic appraisal that the
geopolitical and geoeconomic factors do not begin to give
us the flexibility we need in managing a complex country.

Take natural resources. In a wink of the historical
eye, we have moved the power to set price and supply, from
the consuming nations to the producing nations. Supply
availability and price are largely controlled outside the
continental United States. The U.S., which used to set
the price and control the supply of virtually all major
metals and minerals, now sets the price on only iron ore.
OPEC is well known.

Less known, however, are the other cartels which have
been formed recently:

---The seven major bauxite exporters have formed the
International Bauxite association and have significantly
increased their earnings.

---The six leading phosphate-producing countries have
tripled their prices with additional changes likely.

---Four leading copper producers, through the Inter-
governmental Council of Copper Exporting Countries, have
succeeded, at least to date, in the initial steps to
increase their market power.

---Tin producers through the International Tin Agreement, are seeking a 42% increase in the guaranteed price
of tin.

---The leading coffee producers have succeeded,
through stockpile financing agreements and mutual under-
standings, in seizing control of world coffee prices.

---Five of the leading banana producers, through the organization of banana exporting countries, have levied sizeable taxes on banana exports to boost their returns.

---Many other exporters of commodities, including iron ore, mercury, nickel, tungsten, cobalt, natural rubber, tea, and pepper combined in 1974 to put the stamp of respectability on such actions by passing a resolution through the United Nations calling for "all efforts . . . to facilitate the functioning and to further the aims of producer associations, including their joint marketing arrangements."

---The very success of OPEC pushes other countries, who themselves now must pay more for oil, to explore these measures for their own protection. Jamaica, for instance, has increased the price of bauxite approximately the same amount it has to pay out for petroleum products under the new pricing.

American investments in foreign countries are becoming increasingly subject to nationalization. A recent United Nations survey showed that 875 enterprises in 62 countries were nationalized or otherwise taken over from their original investors between 1960 and 1974. Mines and oil properties were numerically in the minority, but they represented the overwhelming proportion in terms of value and these were largely American-owned. Almost one-fourth of all new investment by U.S. firms now takes place overseas and foreign investment provides a rough equivalent share of U.S. profits.

Dramatic changes in mineral availability are taking place before our very eyes, which will have profound impact on our foreign policy, our domestic policy, our economic system and our lifestyles.

There is thus a message coming out of the West which is not anti-science but also does not reflect the hubris that science and technology can "solve" our pressing problems. Our forefathers lived with the limitations of nature--many of which limits were magnificently expanded by reclamation projects, irrigation, cultivation practices, fertilizers.

Now, however, we start to see clearly that we need to learn also to stay within the albeit expanded limits of nature. At the very least--the constraints of energy, of water, of soil salinity, or receding equifiers and of our natural systems cry "caution." The ghosts of the Mesa Verde Indians increasingly haunt us.

I find great sadness when I see on your program the title "Science: The Key to Our Political Future." There is not <u>one</u> key--but many. To believe there is one key will place human existence on too slender a support system. We, like the Greeks, will lose what we have through hubris.

Abraham Lincoln said during the Civil War: "As our case is new--so must we think and act anew. We must disenthrall ourselves."

I believe we must disenthrall ourselves from the conceitful notion that "Science is THE key to our political future." It is only one key and likely not the major one. The social innovations are as important or more important than the scientific ones. We must reform human systems and values. We must make as many discoveries in inner space as we do in outer space.

"The future is shocking and man's survival is in jeopardy," wrote Harlan Cleveland in a stimulating little book entitled <u>The Future Executive</u>, published in 1972. "Disaster so predictable," he continued, "suggests a sav-ior--to build an ark, to lead us out of the wilderness, to revise our aspirations and revive our faith. But it is in the nature of complexity that no one savior will do. The requirement is for multiple Messiahs. . . men and women whose function is to bring people together to make something happen in the public interest."

2

Toward Increasing Competence of Thought in Public Policy Formation

Kenneth R. Hammond

It is slowly, surely and painfully becoming clear that the human race is coming face-to-face with problems it may not be able to solve. With growing frequency, politicians (for example, Governor Lamm) and scientists in government offices (for example, Joseph Coates) who are attempting to cope with contemporary problems convey to us a grave view of the future; they imply that solutions to our problems may be beyond our problem-solving capacities. And that is the topic I will address in this chapter. How competent is the thought that our policy makers and scientific advisors can bring to bear on such critical problems as the production and distribution of food, energy, and terrifying weapons? If, as more and more people are beginning to suspect, our cognitive competence is less than what is required, then it is time to assess that competence, ask whether it must be increased, and, if so, how this can best be accomplished.

In order to answer these questions, we must consider first the quality of thought that is now applied to policy formation. In what follows, I shall contend that:

(i) Policy makers and their science advisors use a very weak, incompetent mode of thought when forming public policy; therefore, change to a more competent mode of thought is imperative.

(ii) More competent modes of thought are now available to policy makers and their consulting scientists; therefore, they should be used.

(iii) If more competent modes of thought were to be used, the policy making process could be improved, and more effective problem-solving might well occur.

(iv) It is essential that careful attention be given
to the question of whether policy makers can learn from one
instance to the next. Very different consequences will
arise from under- and overestimating the ability of policy
makers to learn from the information they are supplied with.

Each of these topics is discussed. First, however, we
consider the need for analyzing the quality of thought currently used in the policy making process.

The Need for Analysis of the Quality of Thought Used in the Policy Making Process

The cognitive activity of the scientist is treated by
scientists and philosophers as if it were a tender and
precious matter, as indeed it may be. Why shouldn't the
cognitive activity of the policy maker receive equal respect
and equally careful study? The policy maker's task of integrating scientific information into the fabric of social
values is an extraordinarily difficult task, for which there
is no textbook, no handbook, no operating manual, no equip-
ment, no algorithm, no set of heuristics, no theory, not
even a tradition. Young scientists learning their trade
have all of those advantages, all of those supports for
successful cognition. But young policy makers learning
their trade have none of them; each effort to integrate
scientific facts and social values starts fresh, as if it
had never been attempted before. Is there an ancient Greek
philosopher who would be startled to discover that Governor
Lamm finds politicians concerned with "survivability" rather
than application of scientific knowledge to social problems?
Is there an ancient Greek philosopher who would be impressed
by advances in modern political thought?

Senator Pastore's appeal to scientists to "give it to
me straight" (1) regarding the risks created by nuclear
submarines provides an example (in addition to those given
by Governor Lamm) of how helpless modern policy makers feel
when confronted by scientific and technological change:

> As we agonize over these problems, what do we do?
> When a man is sick he goes to see his doctor. He
> does not try to cure himself because, after all, he
> has not had the training. When we . . . want to get
> the best advice on subjects we ourselves have not
> been trained for, what do we do? We go to the ex-
> perts . . . . So, in this moment, what does John
> Pastore do? He looks for the expert. To whom does

he turn? He turns to the father of the nuclear Navy,
Admiral Rickover . . . his name will be immortal when
American history is written . . . So, this morning
. . . . I telephoned "Rick," as I call him, and I said,
"Admiral, on the Trident, give it to me, and give it to
me straight."

If that naked appeal for help seems embarrassing or
funny, scientists might ask themselves what they expect
Senator Pastore to do, if not to ask someone to give it to
him "straight." How is he supposed to think when confronted with conflicting testimony regarding a variety of
unfamiliar topics with which he cannot possibly achieve
competence? How is he expected to introduce coherence into
conflicting scientific information and conflicting social
values? Would it not be fair for Senator Pastore (1) to
say, "If you scientists think what I said was funny or stu-
pid, just how would you do it?" The Senator might also ask,
"Isn't it time scientists gave some scientific attention
to the thinking of people who are, after all, their colleagues in the effort to make science work for the common
good?"

Because I believe that there is no more important matter before the scientific community, I urge that scientists
give their close attention to the analysis of policy makers'
thought. What is it like now? How can scientific work improve it? What is the best we can hope for? And to what
extent will our very best be able to cope with the problems
involved in managing life on earth?

In what follows, I shall place the cognitive activity
of the policy maker in six broad categories in order to
understand better the context in which the policy makers
(and their scientific advisors) must think, and what can be
done to make matters better.

A Matrix of Modes of Inquiry

A Matrix of Modes of Inquiry is presented in Figure 1.
It places six such modes in the context of six continuous
dimensions as follows:

(i) modes of thought, running from analytical to intuitive thought;

(ii) degree of manipulation or control of variables by
policy makers or scientists;

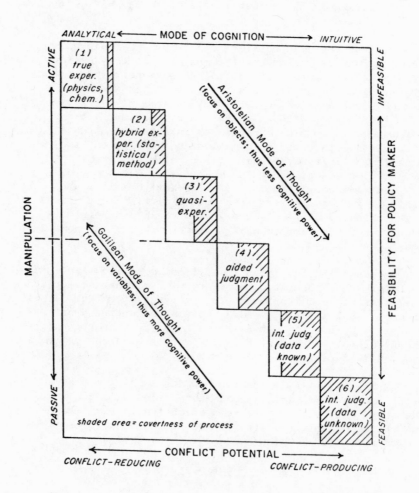

Figure 1.   Modes of Inquiry.

(iii) <u>feasibility</u> of the use of each mode of inquiry with regard to social problems;

(iv) the extent to which a given mode of inquiry is <u>conflict-reducing</u> or <u>conflict-producing</u>;

(v) the <u>covertness</u> of the cognitive activity in each mode;

(vi) the extent to which each mode of inquiry is <u>Galilean</u> (focus on variables) or <u>Aristotelian</u> (focus on objects) in form. It is important to note that a Galilian mode of thought that focuses on variables (e.g., time, distance, etc.) is far more powerful and carries much more potential for intellective, rational, conflict-reduction and problem-solution than Aristotelian object-focused thought (Lewin [2]).

Modes of Inquiry Described

Mode 1 (Strong Analytical Experimentation) refers to the form of inquiry typified by the traditional laboratory experiment carried out by physical scientists.

Mode 2 (Moderately Strong Analytical Experimentation) refers to the experiments that are carried out by biologists, psychologists, sociologists, as well as educational and agricultural researchers. Because this random-assignment experimental-control-group method is based on the logic of statistical inference, it involves elements of judgment not present in the traditional experiments in the physics laboratory and is therefore a less powerful mode of inquiry than Mode 1.

Mode 3 (Weak Analytical Experimentation) refers to the quasi-experiments (and surveys) carried out by social scientists (and others) when strict random assignment, double-blind, pre-post test experiments are not feasible. Such "quasi-experiments" thus fail to meet the criteria demanded by Mode 2 for the application of statistical logic and require more judgment on the part of the inquirer. Mode 3, therefore, provides the weakest mode of active, manipulative, analytical inquiry.

The shaded area in each box in Fig. 1 indicates that a covert judgment process is involved in each mode of inquiry, note that it grows larger from the true experiments of Mode 1 to the weak experiments of Mode 3. Once <u>active</u>

manipulation of variables (such as assignment of people to
one group or another, and/or a systematic change in conditions) is reduced to the point where covert judgmental cognitive activity becomes more important than the manipulation
of variables, an important cognitive boundary has been
crossed (as indicated by the dashed horizontal line in Fig.
1). The shaded area in Box 4 is larger than the unshaded
area, thus indicating that judgment occupies a larger
role in this mode of inquiry than the manipulation of
conditions. For this reason Mode 4 is labelled Strong
Quasi-rational Judgment.

The cognitive activity that takes place in Mode 4 does
not have the weak analytical power of Mode 3 because judgment is required to cope with a variety of variables whose
causal relations have not been separated by active, experimental manipulation. Inability to hold certain variables
constant, and to manipulate other variables leaves the
question of causal directions ambiguous. As a result, inter-
dependent variables must be disentangled sheerly by cognitive activity, that is, by reaching a judgment about what
the results of disentanglement might be. And therein lies
the reason why Mode 4 is a weaker mode of inquiry than Mode
3. For the disentanglement of causal relations by (passive)
cognition instead (active) experimentation is subject to a
variety of psychological factors, such as memory loss, information overload, and recency and primacy effects, to mention only a few. The operation of such psychological factors means that cognitive activity in Mode 4 is quasi-
rational at best.

Mode 4 is the strongest of the quasi-rational modes of
cognition, however, because in this Mode, aids to cognition
are or, at least, can be, employed. These aids reduce the
effects of psychological factors such as those just mentioned as well as many others (see, for example, Slovic's
chapter this volume; see also Slovic, Fischhoff, and
Lichtenstein [3] for a review). Thus, Mode 4 (Strong
Quasi-rational Judgment) refers to the cognitive activity
of persons aided in three ways:

(i) conventional statistical analysis (e.g., compu-
tation of averages, variation and correlation);

(ii) computer simulation of environmental circumstances
(e.g., computer models of the activity of river basins, of
the activity of the economy, of institutions, or even of the
world as, for example, in "Limits to Growth" (4); see
Greenberger, Crenson and Crissey (5) for an overview);

(iii) analyses of judgment and decision such as those developed by Raiffa (6), Keeney and Raiffa (7) Peterson (8), Gardiner and Edwards (9), Hammond (10); see also Zeleny (11), Hammond, Stewart, Brehmer, and Steinmann (12).

Conventional statistical analysis (as described above) has been used as an aid to help policy makers in their thinking for a long time; it is inconceivable that modern government could function without this aid. Yet it is not wholly satisfactory; it does not go far enough. Statistical records remain records of what has happened, and policy makers need to know what will happen. Conventional statistical analysis does not provide assistance in ascertaining cause and effect, and that is what policy makers need to know; what will happen if this course of action is taken rather than that one. The dissatisfaction with the inability of statistical analysis to manipulate conditions, together with the startling capacity of the electronic computer to do so rapidly, has led to the use of computer models to manipulate conditions hypothetically.

Computer simulation of environmental systems can provide an invaluable aid to decision makers because it allows the decision maker to manipulate variables in a hypothetical world, and to observe the outcomes of such manipulations without suffering the consequences of mistaken policies undertaken in a real world. (As has been said elsewhere, "we should let our ideas die in our stead.") As mentioned earlier (memory loss, information overload, etc.) will viate the potential gains acquired by the use of computer models as decision aids for the policy maker. What is required, therefore, in addition to decision aids regarding the environment, is a means for externalizing the processes of judgment. The judgment and decision analyst provides such externalization by quantifying the weights, utilities, functional relations, and aggregation functions used in making a decision. As a result, covertness is decreased, the potential for misunderstanding and conflict is decreased, and most important, an opportunity to focus on variables rather than objects is provided (see Fig. 1).

It is for these reasons Mode 4 is labeled the Strong Quasi-rational Mode. It provides the best form of cognition short of actual manipulation and control of variables together with empirical observation of results. These new aids to cognition provide the first new mode of thought for mankind since the introduction of the mathematics of statistical inference in the eighteenth century.

Mode 5 (Moderately Strong Quasi-rational Thought) refers to the cognitive activity of persons who base their decisions on a known, delimited set of data, but who must act on those data largely in a passive and intuitive fashion; physicians practicing clinical medicine provide an example, as do weather forecasters. Clinical inference is a weaker mode of cognitive activity than aided judgment for the reasons explained above; without such aids, persons are subject to psychological factors of which they are largely unaware, and over which they have little control. Moreover, as indicated in Fig. 1, increased covertness means greater potential for conflict; greater object-focus means a less powerful mode of inquiry.

Mode 6 (Weak Quasi-rational Thought) represents the kind of thought most of us engage in most of the time. It involves an uncertain data base, no manipulation of variables, no statistical controls, and inconsistent logical rules never made explicit. Because it depends wholly on the covert judgment process this common mode of quasi-rational thought is, of course, particularly vulnerable to the effects of numerous psychological factors and therefore it is methodologically very weak. Moreover, under these conditions, no one (not even the person making the judgment) can be sure of what the judgment process is. Therefore, it carries the greatest potential for conflict. In short, Mode 6 is not only the weakest means for solving problems, it is the most dangerous one.

Most important, Mode 6 is oriented toward objects rather than variables; thus it is Aristotelian rather than Galilean. That is why classical Greek philosophers would be perfectly at home in a discussion with Governor Lamm regarding virtually any current public policy problem. Both would focus on this plan for desegration, rather than that one; the choice of this form of energy use, rather than that one, and so on. In short, no change in the mode of thought applied to problems of social .policy. Greek scientists, however, would not find themselves equally at home with modern scientists, not merely because modern scientists know so much more, but because they employ a wholly different, variable-oriented mode of cognition that was given great prominence by Galileo. That is, Galileo did not ask which objects behaved in which ways; rather, he asked how variables such as time and distance affected the behavior of all objects. The critical task for scientists, then, is to free policy makers from the object-focused mode of cognition they currently use, to the more powerful one that is oriented toward variables. Can that be done?

Before answering that question we provide an example of how
a social problem moves through the Matrix of Modes of Inquiry.

Consider the question of permitting a new drug to be
used by physicians. First, Mode 1 (Strong Analytical
Experimentation) is employed to discover the molecular
structure of the chemical agent in question as well as its
behavior in the presence of other chemical agents. Mode 2
(Moderately Strong Analytical Experimentation) is then employed in animal experiments and clinical trials involving
random assignment of subjects to experimental and control
groups with appropriate pre- and post-test (and perhaps continuous) measurements. Mode 3 (Weak Analytical Experimentation) is employed when subsequent (i.e., post-marketing) data
regarding the effects of the drug are required. Random assignment of subjects and pre- and post-testing cannot be
achieved. And although the resulting data are by no means
useless, they must be interpreted, that is, judgment must
be employed, in order to reach a conclusion; therefore dispute over the meaning of the data is not only frequent but
vigorous. Mode 4, in which aids to judgment make a strong
form of quasi-rational thought possible, has not yet been
employed in the process of deciding whether a drug is
efficacious and safe to use. Mode 5 (Moderately Strong
Quasi-rational Thought) is used during clinical trials with
patients (its function there is to appraise, that is, judge
the progress of patients), or in the epidemiological (post-
marketing) studies of Mode 3. In both cases, the data upon
which the judgment is based may be known, but the manner in
which the data are used by physicians as they exercise their
clinical judgment will not be (for an example, see Stewart,
Joyce and Lindell [13]). Because the latter modes of
thought involve considerable covert cognitive activity, a
dispute is likely to arise as to the safety or efficacy of
the drug. A public hearing will then be held, and Mode 6
(Weak Quasi-rational Thought) will be applied. At this
point, all varieties of data and judgment will be applied
and the chaos of dispute will follow. In Coates' words a
"problem" will have become an "issue."

The course of the scientific development and of the
swine flu vaccine and the development of public policy to
vaccinate tens of millions of persons provides an example
of the use of each mode of inquiry. The final decision to
discontinue the use of the vaccine provides a classical
example of the confusion and chaos of the weak, quasi-
rational, conflict-ridden thought of Mode 6. No one will

ever be able to retrace the cognitive processes that led
to an action that affected the health of millions of people.

Can this general deterioration of cognition activity
be halted at some point before it reaches the weakness of
Modes 5 and 6, and thus reduces our cognitive competence
to the point of inadequacy and failure? That question is
considered next.

What Is the Most Powerful Form of Inquiry That Policy Makers and Science Advisors Can Use?

Which of these six modes of inquiry can best be applied to policy formation? If the most powerful form of
inquiry, the strong analytical thought of Mode 1, could be
brought to bear on Senator Pastore's policy question or
policy questions like it (e.g., "should we permit
recombinant DNA research?") it would be most desirable to
do so. But questions like these cannot be answered in the
physics laboratory. Nor can they be answered by the moderately strong analytical procedures of Mode 2. Indeed, the
results produced by the typical random assignment study in
Mode 2 have seldom produced information that policy makers
can use, for reasons that Coates makes clear in chapter 2.

Facing the loss of the moderate analytical power of
Mode 2, Campbell (14) and others have advocated the next
best mode of inquiry, the weak analytical mode (3) that
employs quasi-experiments. Although quasi-experiments
lack rigor, and thus produce information of less certain
validity than Mode 2 experiments, they are feasible, and
many quasi-experiments have been carried out (see Boruch
and Riecken [15]). But the weakness of the information
requires that policy makers exercise their judgment to a
large degree; quasi-experiments are not highly valuable as
aids to decision makers.

Note from Fig. 1 that if the weak analytical power of
Mode 3 cannot be employed because conditions cannot be
changed or manipulated, then our best recourse must be to
the strong form of quasi-rational thought of Mode 4. In
this mode policy makers are aided in the exercise of their
judgment by the three methods indicated above: conventional
statistical description, computer simulation of environmental or other (e.g., econometric) systems, and decision
and judgment analysis. These quantitative aids to quasi-
rational judgment should be provided for policy makers because such aids to judgment increase the rationality of the

judgment process and reduce its covertness. The use of such aids is entirely feasible in policy making (for a recent example, see Hammond and Adelman, chapter 8). And when quasi-experiments of Mode 3 can be performed, the strong form of quasi-rational thought provided by aids to cognition can be applied to the dubious results of the weak analytical quasi-experiments of Mode 3, and the power of inquiry improved. In short, Modes 3 and 4 can be used together in a way that strengthens both.

Mode 5 (Weak Quasi-rational Thought) is, of course, highly feasible, and can be applied to any delimited set of data. Mode 5 is now being applied to social indicators (16) (variables that are used to indicate the "social health" of the nation). This "clinical" mode of cognition lacks the quasi-rational power of Mode 4, however, because it lacks the rationality provided by the cognitive aids that not only reduce the effects of psychological factors but externalize them, and thus make retraceable the nature of the judgment process applied to the indicators; judgments regarding "social health" (or the output of simulations) are as subjective as in the case of clinical medicine. The same holds true for the subjective judgments that must be made if the complex and confusing outputs of computer simulations (such as those seen in "Limits to Growth" [4]) are unloaded onto the policy maker. (See Hammond, Mumpower, and Smith [17] for an example of the advantages that accrue from a computer model of the environment together with the techniques of judgment analysis.) Weak as Mode 5 may be, the use of a known, delimited set of data in the form of objective indicators is a vast improvement over the weak quasi-rational cognitive activity of Mode 6.

In Mode 6 we find what should be the cognitive activity of last resort; unhappily, it is often the cognitive activity of first resort. Only when all else fails, when all recourse to more analytical, more powerful modes of thought have been found to be unfeasible, should the weakest mode of cognition (unaided human judgment based on an unknown set of data) be employed. Yet anyone who observes policy makers at work will recognize at once that weak quasi-rational thought (Mode 6) is their typical form of cognitive activity, for the simple reason that it is feasible. Of course, scientists, whose typical mode of cognition involves the strong or moderate forms of analytical thought of Modes 1 or 2 are quick to detect the "sloppy thinking" typical of Mode 6, and are scornful of it. Indeed, anyone who has heard scientists discuss the process of policy formation knows that scientists believe that if only policy makers were exposed to the

discipline of the strong form of analytical thought so successfully employed in Mode 1, most of the problems of policy
formation would disappear.

Self-satisfying as that belief may be, when scientists
serve as advisors to policy makers, their first resort is
also to the incompetent cognitive activity of Mode 6. One
can be no more certain about the boundaries of the data set
being employed by the scientist in his role as consultant
than they can be about the information being employed by
the policy maker. Nor can one be any more certain about the
cognitive process that the scientist uses to organize the
fuzzily-bound information upon which his judgment is based.
When scientists offer advice regarding the safety of recombinant DNA research, nuclear sources of energy, the effects
of busing, mass vaccination, and the like, they are forced
to move from the strong analytical modes of cognition (upon
which their intellectual authority rests) to the weak, quasi-
rational form of cognition of Mode 5 (at best) and/or Mode 6
(at worst). In short, the cognitive activity employed by
scientists in Mode 6 is just as covertly judgmental and thus
just as mysterious, nonanalytical, and thus conflict-pro-
ducing, as that employed by policy makers or anyone else who
employs Mode 6.

Some readers may find the general categorization of
cognition in Fig. 1 acceptable yet doubt these assertions
about the weakness of the cognitive activity of policy makers and scientists in their role as advisors to them. For-
tunately, no one needs to accept my assertions on faith, for
both policy makers and scientists have spoken plainly on
these matters themselves. Indeed, policy makers who write
their memoirs often take pains to point out how whimsical
the policy making process is. Somehow after retirement
they appear to feel duty-bound to disabuse us of the false
notion that anything better than the incompetent, intuitive,
chaotic Mode 6 is put to work in high circles, although
their pronouncements before retirement would have us believe
that the use of anything less than the pure analytical
thought of Mode 1 would be regarded with disdain.

Consider this description of the planning process in
the State Department provided by George Kennan (18), perhaps the outstanding scholar of the diplomatic corps in the
20th century:

I have a largish farm in Pennsylvania . . . . The farm
includes two hundred thirty-five acres, and a number of
buildings. On every one of those acres, I have

discovered, things are constantly happening. Weeds are
growing. Gullies are forming. Fences are falling
down. Paint is fading. Wood is rotting. Insects are
burrowing. Nothing seems to be standing still. The
days . . . pass in a . . . succession of alarms and
excursions. Here a bridge is collapsing. No sooner
do you start to repair it than a neighbor comes to complain about a hedgerow which you haven't kept up--a
half-mile away on the other side of the farm. At that
very moment your daughter arrives to tell you that
someone left the gate to the hog pasture open and the
hogs are out. On the way to the hog pasture you discover that the beagle hound is happily liquidating one
of the children's pet kittens. In burying the kitten
you look up and notice that a whole section of the barn
roof has been blown off, and needs instant repair.
Somebody shouts pitifully from the bathroom window that
the pump must have busted--there's no water in the
house. At that moment a truck arrives with five tons
of stone for the lane. And as you stand helplessly
there, wondering which of these crises to attend to
first, you notice the farmer's little boy standing
silently before you with that maddening smile that is
halfway a leer, and when you ask him what's up, he says
triumphantly, "The bull's busted out and he's eating
the strawberry bed."

That description of chaos (delivered to the War College!) may lead scientists to say, "Just as I thought." But
now the memoirs of George Kistiakowsky, Eisenhower's science
advisor, and a man of high repute in both scientific and
governmental circles, are available, and we may examine
these in order to discover to what extent the strong analytical mode of thought (Mode 1) is applied to decisions affecting public policy. Again, to spare you from my own
interpretations, I quote from Scoville's review (19) of
Kistiakowsky's memoirs. Scoville, who was Assistant Director for Science and Technology for the CIA during Kistiakowsky's tenure as science advisor, and who indicates that
he worked very closely with Kistiakowsky, has this to say
about the use of analytical thought (Mode 1) by Kistiakowsky:

Kistiakowsky's book will quickly disillusion anyone
who has assumed that scientific decisions related to
national policy are carefully developed on the basis
of rigorous scientific principles and procedures to
produce an incontrovertible solution to the problem at

at hand. Policy-making by scientists is no more pre-
cise then policy-making by politicians, economists,
or diplomats.

In short, policy makers and science advisors are tel-
ling us that public policy is formed by the weakest mode of
thought.

As might be expected under these circumstances, neither
consultant nor policy maker develop high regard for the contribution of the other, nor for the contributions of their
colleagues on the same side of the fence; memoirs from both
diplomats and scientists indicate strong doubts about the
intellectual capabilities of their peers as well as their
opposite numbers. Nor can we expect such mutual disappoint-
ment to disappear unless and until stronger modes of inquiry
that include decreased covertness of thought and increased
availability of conflict-reducing mechanisms are made available to policy makers and scientists in their effort to form
public policy. The constantly reiterated hope that better
policy will be forthcoming by changing the personalities involved in forming policy is a false and misleading hope that
should be abandoned; our best hope for the future lies not
in new personalities but in changing the present incompetent
mode of inquiry to a more powerful, less covert, less con-
flict-producing one. The future is too dangerous, too precarious, to be left to personalities, however colorful,
however awesome their past achievement, or however appealing
their homely simplicity; imprisonment in Mode 6 makes personality irrelevant. And although incompetence may be more
tolerable when combined with rectitude than with villainy,
in the end, failure remains failure.

Can we escape from the exigencies of Mode 6? Can policy makers move from the weak, poorly analytical, conflict-
producing Modes 5 and 6 to the stronger quasi-rational
thought of Mode 4? Virtually all judgment and decision
researchers believe that it is possible to employ aids to
decision making that would make the move to Mode 4 possible
now. And systems analysts who develop simulations of environmental systems believe and have demonstrated that these
aids to cognition can be usefully employed now.

If the answer to the question of whether we can escape
from Modes 5 and 6 is yes, the next question must be, will
we? Possibly not. The reason for doubt lies in the fact
that policy makers and scientists are skeptical of the

value of decision aids. Nearly all are convinced of the
power of their own wisdom--before they write their memoirs,
at least. Few policy makers are as willing to reveal their
helplessness as is Senator Pastore, and few scientists are
eager to acknowledge that the analytical power of Mode 1 is
not always with them. Virtually everyone overestimates the
power of his or her use of Mode 6; indeed, few have ever
considered an alternative to it.

This is not the place to inquire into the reasons why
humanity must suffer the consequences of using weak modes of
thought long after it has been demonstrated that stronger
modes of thought are available. Rather, we turn to the more
important question of what can be expected from the use of
more competent modes of inquiry by policy makers when policy
makers choose to use them.

Consequences of Over- and Under-estimating Our Cognitive Ability

Must policy makers and their societies endure forever
the incompetence, the haplessness and mistrust created by
the weakness of cognition in Modes 5 and 6? Will the
world's social and physical systems be forever insensitive
to the application of the confused policies that are produced by cognitive incompetence? The answer to the first
question must be "no," we cannot continue to endure incompetent modes of thought because the answer to the second
is certainly "no," the world's social and physical systems
will not forever be resilient to the application of poor
policies. Moreover, there is no doubt that the advantages
of Mode 4 can be acquired now; quantitative aids for judgment have been used on many occasions in the public and
private sector. (See Hammond and Adelman, this volume;
Gardiner and Edwards [9]; Keeney and Raiffa [7]; Howard [20]
for examples of the use of aided judgment in public policy
formation; see also Boruch and Riecken [15].) But, how
valuable are the decision aids of Mode 4? What can and
cannot be expected of them?

The answer is that at present no one knows what the
limit of our cognitive ability is with regard to forming
social policies to cope with our problems; moreover, it may
be impossible to find out. Under these circumstances, the
best step to take now is to evaluate the likelihood and
consequences of mistakes. That is, in the absence of
knowledge, or even good estimates, of our cognitive abilities under a variety of circumstances, we should consider

the likelihood and consequences of two errors: (a) making
the mistake of <u>overestimating</u> our abilities, and (b) making
the mistake of <u>underestimating</u> them.

First, consider what has been claimed for the value of
the weak, analytical, quasi-experiments of Mode 3.   Campbell
and others (e.g., Boruch and Riecken [<u>15</u>]; Caplan and Nelson
[<u>21</u>]) argue that if Mode 3 can be implemented, <u>learning</u> will
take place.   That is, if Mode 3 were to be implemented, policy makers would learn from the results of quasi-experiments
and, therefore, society would become increasingly effective
in solving its problems.

This is hardly a striking suggestion, until one notes that
Campbell and others believe that <u>learning is contingent upon</u>
<u>achieving Mode 3</u>.   That contingency implies that they be-
lieve learning does <u>not</u> take place <u>now</u>, since the quasi-
experiments of Mode 3 are seldom employed.   Since Modes 5
and 6 have <u>always</u> been predominant, it follows that society's policy makers have <u>never</u> been able to learn.   Therefore, only if Mode 3 quasi-experiments are employed will
they be able to learn.   Before accepting that conclusion,
the reader should consider the consequences of being wrong.

Consider first the error of <u>under</u>estimating the power
of Mode 3 and thus falsely believing that we could not learn
from them.   In this case we would falsely believe that we
could not learn general principles from quasi-experiments;
that quasi-experiments provided only situation-specific results and allowed no extrapolation to similar events.   Would
that error be harmful?   Yes, of course it would.   The error
of underestimating the value of Mode 3 would unnecessarily
prevent us from learning; it would keep us from correcting
our mistakes, and therefore, we would not be realizing our
potential to make matters better.   Campbell has strongly
advocated the use of Mode 3 quasi-experiments, because he
believes we are in danger of making this error now.

Now consider the error of <u>overestimating</u> the power of
Mode 3 quasi-experiments, assuming that policy makers <u>could</u>
learn from quasi-experiments when they could <u>not</u>.   The error
of overestimating the power of any mode of inquiry needs very
close attention, because virtually everyone believes that
societies and their policy makers <u>can</u> learn, even <u>without</u>
Mode 3 quasi-experiments; therefore it is an error that has
a high likelihood of being undetected.   The following quotation (taken from Pressman and Wildavsky [<u>22</u>, p. 125]) is
typical of policy analysts' views on this matter and represents what most people believe:

Organizations, which deal with the collective efforts
of men, are devoted to the processing of information
and the generation of knowledge. Their ability to
test the environment so as to correct error and reinforce truth makes them effective. Inability to learn
is _fatal_ (italics ours).

Because such views are generally accepted, we are therefore much more likely to make the error of overestimating
the limits of achievement in Mode 3 (believing policy makers
can learn when, in fact, they cannot). Because the likelihood of this error is high, I turn briefly to an examination
of three conditions that must hold if policy makers are to
learn generalizable principles under the most feasible form
of experimentation--Mode 3 quasi-experiments. My purpose in
identifying these prerequisites is to emphasize the possibility that policy makers may _not_ be able to learn from Mode
3 quasi-experiments.

Prerequisite 1: Modes of inquiry weaker than Mode 3
must be prohibited by someone, somehow. Most important, if
Modes 5 and 6 are permitted, false principles cannot be dis-
proved, and therefore learning will not occur. But it is
obvious that this prerequisite cannot be enforced; there is
no imaginable institution that can drive Modes 5 and 6 out
of use.

Prerequisite 2: Results of quasi-experiments _must_ be
accepted; alternative hypotheses, however plausible they may
appear to the person who holds them, must be relinquished.
If they are not, false hypotheses will not be discarded and
will continue to guide action. But of course the dubious
results of quasi-experiments will not cause policy makers
to relinquish plausible hypotheses and there is no imaginable institution that could force them to do so; as a result, learning will not occur.

Prerequisite 3: Learning requires circumstances in
which learning _can_ occur. But quasi-experiments provide
only highly uncertain outcomes, and therefore, they evoke
subjective judgments regarding uncertain events. Research
on learning to improve one's judgment in tasks involving
multiple criteria and uncertain outcomes shows clearly and
definitely that persons are poor learners in these situations (see Hammond et al. [12]). Unless the task is very,
very simple, learning will not occur under these circumstances.

In sum, although Mode 3 offers the best hope for making learning possible, it is very doubtful that the prerequisites for learning can be achieved in Mode 3. Yet, warnings that the "inability to learn is fatal" are announced frequently (although the possibility that policy makers may be unable to learn is never examined). And exhortations to learn, based on the unquestioned assumption that learning can oc- cur, are also commonplace. Thus, for example, Hitch (23) insists that in order to cope with the "energy dilemma . . . We must have a plan that can . . . be adjusted frequently as we learn." But there is no evidence that Hitch has any plans for making learning possible, or indeed, whether he has ever examined and set forth the conditions that are nec- essary for making learning possible.

If it is true, or even only probably true, that the quasi-experiments of Mode 3 will not make learning possible, we should give careful attention to the practical conse- quences of making the error of believing that we can learn when, in fact, we cannot. For example, if a society falsely believed that it could learn, how could it ever discover that it could not? And if a society persisted in falsely believing it could learn, think of the time and resources that would be wasted in the vain effort to learn. Think of the time wasted on false accusations of stupidity and ineptness when anticipated learning did not occur. Think of the accusations of stupidity and ineptness that occur now, as people are charged with failing to learn "the lessons of Viet Nam" or, more generally, "the lessons of history" when, in fact, not even the weak analytical power of Mode 3 was available to make such learning possible. In short, the error of falsely believing that society does have the methodological means to produce learning could have effects that are just as severe as falsely believing that society does not have the means for learning. Note, however, that the likelihood of falsely believing that policy makers can learn is far larger than the error of falsely believing that they cannot learn.

Now apply the same approach to Mode 4; suppose we make the error of underestimating the power of Mode 4. That is, suppose we assume that aids to judgment will not enable us to achieve greater rationality when in fact they would. That error would lead us to reject their use and would force us to rely on Modes 5 and 6 when reliance on these weak modes of inquiry was unnecessary. Would that error be harm- ful? Indeed it would; the cognitive activity of policy

makers and their scientific advisors would be no better than
it is now. That conclusion leaves no room for optimism
about the future of a species that now has so many uncon-
trolled means for devastation of the earth.

The alternative error--overestimating the power of the
strong quasi-rational thought of Mode 4--appears to be a
benign error relative to any of the other errors. For if
we assumed that greater rationality could be achieved
through the use of the quantitative methods of Mode 4 when,
in fact, greater rationality could not be achieved, we would
be no worse off than if we had continued to employ Modes 5
and 6. Neither time nor energy would be lost, inasmuch as
the use of Modes 5 and 6 consumes vast quantities of time
with little success. Yet it may well be that the overestimation of the power of Mode 4 could lead to the same sort
of recrimination that we now observe with regard to the
overestimation of Modes 5 and 6.

Overestimating the power of Modes 5 and 6 appears to be
our most likely, and most costly, folly. It has long been
assumed that these are the most powerful modes of thought
available to policy makers and that they are powerful
enough, that they are sufficient for their purpose. Only
recently has it become apparent that they very well may not
be.

It is important to observe that asymmetrical criteria
are usually employed when Mode 4 is compared with Modes 5
and 6. The procedures for aiding judgment are required to
be perfect; any flaw, real or imagined, is sufficient to
reject their use, whereas the judgment processes of Modes
5 and 6 escape criticism altogether as modes of inquiry;
they escape because of their long practice and because they
are identified (uncritically) as "wisdom." But the burden
of proof with regard to any preference now lies equally
upon the advocate of any choice; it is no longer simply a
matter of rejecting Mode 4 with the verdict: "perfection
not proven." The advantages and disadvantages and imper-
fections of each mode of thought, together with the dangers
of over and underestimating their power must be considered.
Mode 4 need not be infallible in order to be chosen over
Modes 5 and 6, it needs only to be better.

An example of the danger of overestimating the unaided
cognitive powers of highly placed political leaders by
their counterparts can be seen in the remarks of the President of Mexico (Lopez Portillo) (24) after his recent visit
with the President of the United States: "Carter has the

gift of seeing the problems of finance, trade, technology, and immigration in relation to one another." But it is easy to demonstrate the fact that no human being operating within the weak quasi-rational Modes 5 and 6 can do that. No human begin operating in Modes 5 and 6 can do what the President of Mexico expects the President of the United States to do (and we may expect to discover this from President Carter's memoirs, but not before). If the President of Mexico does indeed believe that the President of the United States does have the mysterious "gift" of superhuman cognitive power, he will be disappointed.

Unfortunately, President Carter's inevitable failure to see "the problems of finance, trade, technology, and immigration in relation to one another" will be attributed to a failure of will, rather than to the incompetence of a mode of inquiry, because the President of Mexico, like nearly all other human beings, overestimates the cognitive power of Modes 5 and 6. And failures of will usually receive treatment intended to teach the offender a lesson. Thus, overestimating the cognitive power of Mode 6 often leads to punishment for what is assumed to be a failure that could be avoided. In short, international relations are apt to suffer as a result of overestimating the cognitive competence of a political leader restricted to Modes 5 and 6.

To sum up, unless some marked change occurs in the mode of human thought applied to social problems, there is little reason to believe that mankind can manage life of earth any better in the future than in the past. Mistakes will not be fewer, but their consequences will certainly be more severe, possibly to the point of ultimate catastrophe. If these mistakes are to be avoided significant improvement in our cognitive competence needs to be sought and must be achieved.

References and Notes

1. J. Pastore, Congressional Record, 11995 (1972).
2. K. Lewin, Dynamic Theory of Personality (McGraw-Hill, New York, 1935).
3. P. Slovic, B. Fischhoff, S. Lichtenstein, Annual Review of Psychology 28, 1-39 (1977).
4. D.H. Meadows, D.L. Meadows, J. Randers, W.W. Dehrens, The Limits to Growth: A Report for the Club of Rome's Project on the Predicament of Mankind (Universe Books, New York, 1972).

5. M. Greenberger, M. Crenson, B. Crissey, Models in the Policy Process: Public Decision Making in the Computer Era (Russell Sage Foundation, New York, 1976).

6. H. Raiffa, Decision Analysis (Addison-Wesley, Reading, Mass., 1968).

7. R.L. Keeney, H. Raiffa, Decisions with Multiple Objectives: Preferences and Value Tradeoffs (Wiley, New York, 1976).

8. C.R. Peterson, Design and Evaluation of Military Systems (Paper presented at the Meeting of the American Psychological Association, Washington, D.C., 1976).

9. P.C. Gardiner, W. Edwards, in Human Judgment and Decision Processes, M.F. Kaplan and S. Schwartz, Eds. (Academic Press, New York, 1975). .

10. K.R. Hammond, Science 172, 903-908 (1971).

11. M. Zeleny, in Multiple Criteria Decision Making: Kyoto 1975, M. Zeleny, Ed. (Springer-Verlag, Berlin, 1975).

12. K.R. Hammond, T.R. Stewart, B. Brehmer, D. Steinmann, in Human Judgment and Decision Processes, M.F. Kaplan and S. Schwartz, Eds. (Academic Press, New York, 1975).

13. T.R. Stewart, C.R.B. Joyce, M.K. Lindell, in Psychoactive Drugs and Social Judgment: Theory and Research, K.R. Hammond and C.R.B. Joyce, Eds. (Wiley, New York, 1975).

14. D.T. Campbell, American Psychologist 24, 409-429 (1969). See also D.T. Campbell, J.C. Stanley, in Handbook of Research on Teaching, N.L. Gage, Ed. (Rand McNally, Chicago, 1963); Reprinted as Experimental and Quasi-Experimental Designs for Research (Rand McNally, Chicago, 1966).

15. R.F. Boruch, H.W. Riecken, Experimental Testing of Public Policy: The Proceedings of the 1974 Social Science Research Council Conference on Social Experiments (Westview Press, Boulder, Colo., 1975). See also H.W. Riecken, R.F. Boruch, D.T. Campbell, N. Caplan, T.K. Glennan, J.W. Pratt, A. Rees, W. Williams, Social Experiments: A Method for Planning and Evaluating Social Programs (Seminar Press, New York, 1974).

16. See R.A. Bauer, Ed., Social Indicators (Massachusetts Institute of Technology Press, Cambridge, Mass., 1966); E.B. Sheldon, W.E. Moore, Eds., Indicators of Social Change (Russell Sage Foundation, 1968); A. Shonfield, S. Shaw, Eds., Social Indicators and Social Policy (Heinemann Educational Books, London, 1972); D.M. Smith, The Geography of Social Well-Being in the United States (McGraw-Hill, New York, 1973). See also Social Indicators Research (1974-   ).

17. K.R. Hammond, J.L. Mumpower, T.H. Smith, IEEE Transactions, in press.
18. G. Kennan, Memoirs: 1925-1950. (Atlantic, Little & Brown, New York, 1967).
19. H. Scoville, Jr., Science 195, 168 (1977).
20. R.A. Howard, J.E. Matheson, D.W. North, Science 176, 1191-1202 (1972).
21. N. Caplan, S.D. Nelson, American Psychologist 28, 199-211 (1973).
22. J. Pressman, A. Wildavsky, Implementation: How Great Expectations in Washington Are Dashed in Oakland (University of California Press, Berkeley, Calif., 1973).
23. C.J. Hitch, Science 195, 825 (1977).
24. L. Portillo, Denver Post, 20 February 1977.
25. Supported by National Science Foundation grant BNS 76-09560. I thank David Krech, Joseph Coates, and Lawrence Weiss for their reviews of early drafts of this manuscript; I also thank the staff of the Western Institute of Behavioral Science for their help.

3

What Is a
Public Policy Issue?

Joseph F. Coates

Introduction

The American body politic is neither in extremis nor in
crisis, at least in terms analogous to clinical medicine.
That may be unfortunate, since our government is well organized to deal with crises. We have in our history a number
of incredibly effective and marvelous responses to such crises as the great depression, World War II, and scores of
regional disasters.

The nation's situation is substantially different, and
in some sense worse. In a crisis the matter will be over.
The patient will live to recover his health or die, in some
short time. But the troubles of our body politic are deepen-
ing, worsening, and we seem to be only slowly able to come to
manage some of them.

Why is this the situation? Basically, because mechanisms of government and their organization and structure are
obsolete to a degree that has engendered a fundamental built-
in incompetence to deal with many of the new issues which the
nation faces. The issues are new in the sense that they have
come to full flower in the last thirty years. Cut and fit
accommodation and incremental change, the traditional strategies of government, are increasingly ineffective, if not
sterile modes of operation. The very mechanism for safeguard-
ing democracy, overlapping and divided power and checks and
balances are increasingly the source of paralysis, the bane
of leadership and the instruments of fools. Consequently,
one must look to alternative means of probing, analyzing and
enriching policymaking.

The present serious condition of government flows out
of the effects of long-term trends operating in American

TABLE I
LONG-TERM TRENDS FORMING
THE BASIS FOR THE FUTURE*

General Long-Term Societal Trends

1. Economic prosperity, affluence, and inflation
2. Expanding education throughout society
3. Rise of knowledge industries and a knowledge-dependent society
4. Relative decline in common knowledge of the physical world
5. Urbanization/metropolitanization/suburbanization
6. Rise of the middle class society
7. Cultural homogenization—the growth of a national society
8. Growth of permanent military establishment
9. Mobility, a) personal, b) physical, c) occupational, d) job
10. International affairs and national security as a major societal factor

Technology Trends

11. The centrality and increasing dominance of technology in the economy and society
12. Integration of the national economy
13. Integration of the national with the international economy
14. The growth of research and development as a factor in economy
15. High technological turnover rate
16. The development of mass media in telecommunications and printing
17. An awareness of the finitude of resources

Trends in Labor Force and Work

18. Specialization
19. Growth of the service sector
20. Relative decline of primary and secondary employment
21. Growth of information industries, movement toward an information society
22. Expansion of credentialism
23. Women, blacks, and other minority groups entering into the labor force
24. Early retirement
25. Unionism
26. Growth of pensions and pension funds
27. Movement toward second careers and mid-life change in career
28. Decline of the work ethic

Trends in Values and Concerns

29. General shift in societal values
30. Diversity as a growing, explicit value
31. Decline of traditional authority

32. The growth of anti-authoritarian movements
33. Increasing aspirations and expectations of success
34. Growth of tourism, vacationing, and travel
35. General expectations of high level of medical care
36. General expectations of high level of social service
37. The growth of consumerism
38. Growth of physical culture and personal health movements
39. Civil rights, civil liberties expansion for blacks, Chicanos, gays, and other minorities
40. Growth of women's liberation movement

Family Trends

41. Decline in birth rates
42. Shifts in rates of family formation, marriage, divorce, and living styles
43. The growth of leisure
44. The growth of the do-it-yourself movement
45. Improved nutrition with the consequent decline in the age of menarche
46. Protracted adolescence
47. Decline in the number and significance of rights of passage, birth, death, marriage, etc.
48. Isolation of children from the world of adult concern
49. The acculturation of children by other children
50. The growth of a large aged population
51. The replacement of the extended family by the nuclear family and other living arrangements

Institutional Trends

52. The institutionalization of problems. This is the tendency to spawn new institutions and new institutional mechanisms for dealing with what were in the past personal, private, or nongovernmental responsibilities.
53. Bureaucratization of public and private institutions
54. Growth of big government
55. The growth of big business
56. Growth of multi-national corporations
57. Growth of future studies and forecasting and the institutionalization of foresight mechanisms and long-range planning.
58. Growth of public participation in public institution and private institution decision making
59. The growing demands for accountability and the expenditure of public resources
60. Growth of demands for social responsibility.

*"Why Think About the Future: Some Administrative-Political Perspectives," Joseph F. Coates, Public Administration Review, Sept/Oct. 1976, p. 585.

society for forty to sixty years (See Table I). These long-
term trends in a steady continuous evolution have so altered
the technical-economic-social landscape of the United States
that virtually every problem, every issue, every opportunity
has an intrinsic structural character different from seemingly parallel or related issues of one or two generations
ago.

An illustration or two of how long-term trends evolve
and interact to generate new issues may be useful. Referring
to Table 1, Trends 3,45 and 46, one finds the rise of knowledge and information dependent occupations and industries
makes it desirable if not necessary to extend the time that
a child or young person spends in school. Improved nutrition
is physiologically and to some extent psychologically
readying the young person for an adult world just as the
social and economic realities lead to protracted adolescence
and an extended period of economic dependence on the family.
Many of the problems of urban youth flow out of this conflict.
The alienation from schools, questionable curriculum content,
problems in behavior and deportment, dropping-out, the purpose of the junior high school, and the socialization of
young people into adult mores--all become new issues or issues
of added importance derivative of this structural conflict.

As an additional illustration, consider Trends 11, 53
and 58. As our society becomes more technologically inten-
sive as the scale and scope of technological enterprises
increase, there is a natural if not inevitable tendency to
bureaucratize public and private institutions. Large technological enterprises require experts for their administration, management, planning, and care. Bureaucracy is the
home of the expert. On the other hand the growth of public
participation and the push toward broader base involvements
in public and private decisionmaking, in part is stimulated
by the growing concerns about technology and is substantially in conflict with the mores and behavior of bureaucracy.

The purpose of this paper is to explore one small but
important portion of the policy landscape, namely, two
questions: What is a public policy issue? What are some
of the problems associated with bringing the intellectual
resources of the nation to bear on our national issues?
Therefore, some attention will also be given to the question
of the characteristics of an issue and its institutional
environment.

There are numerous areas virtually barren of policy
research, for example, materials, bureaucracy, terrorism and
constitutional reform; and in other areas where there seem to

be legions of investigators concerned with crime, housing, war and urban development, little is produced germane to public policy in the short- or long-term or fruitful in moving public policy discussions forward.   Consequently, this paper is directed at developing a clear and explicit perception of some factors entering into policy research with a view to informing those who would do policy research.

If one is better informed about the implicit and explicit context of policy decisions, one should be able to do more useful and effective work.

Policy is not action. A policy is a statement, either explicit or implicit, directed or derived, as to what are the goals and intentions of a government, a branch of govern-ment, an agency, or some other unit or organization. Policy itself is given meaning and set into action through:

- Policy actions, such as legislation
- Programs
- Projects
- Regulations, taxes and other operations of the instruments of government

It is through these means that government does its work and accomplishes objectives or fails to meet our needs.

Why do these actions of government so consistently fail to achieve their goals and often end up stifling or stymie-ing progress and even causing setbacks?

One basic reason is that we are managing a tightly integrated world of complex networks of society's technical and institutional systems with an information base, and a social control structure, carried over from simpler, slower moving, more provincial times. Two fundamental principles of the operation and stability of complex systems are feed-back and flexibility. Furthermore in our own world, which demands a future orientation, a third fundamental need is forecasting. A systematic look to the future anticipates needs and consequences and can thereby lead to better and more flexible feedback seeking policies and plans.

So, the three principal needs for a healthy, well-functioning body politic are forecasting, feedback, and flexibility. While many requirements exist for the effective functioning of society such as institutions, organizations and shared values, these three Fs requirements are the dominant dynamic factors underlaying the generation and orchestration of knowledge and its effective application in public and private institutions.

Of course in the past, we have always had some form of
these three fundamentals. But the traditional means by which
feedback and flexibility were achieved and the older mechanisms for forecasting are intrinsically obsolescent. They
depended less on interaction and more on disaggregation and
slower responses to changing conditions. The mechanisms
were not premised on a nation in which virtually every important issue and problem is national in scope. But we still
handle them in a multilevel and multiagency framework. There
are 80,000 units of government in the USA.

Deficiencies in the present forecasting and feedback
requirements of much major legislation is shown by the requirements of the environmental impact statements. The
statements present limited forecasts of little decision-
making saliency in an enigmatic format couched in bland
bureaucratese. The feedback loops in the process have
response times matching those of the enterprise itself. The
design and execution of a central power station has been
virtually increased by 30 to 50 percent by these feedback
and forecasting requirements. This attempt at forecasting
feedback instead of being flexible has become so bogged
down in procedure that not only is its flexibility lost but
substance is expurgated.

An even more ubiquitous area of the failure of feedback
and flexibility is in courts and criminal justice systems.
It is now a vanishingly small probability (approximately 3
percent) that any perpetrator of a crime will serve any
significant time incarcerated. The more heinous the crime,
the more prominent the perpetrator, the more generous the
scope and scale of the foul deed, the less likely the mal-
factor is to receive speedy or any other kind of justice.

Public Policy Issues

A public policy issue may be defined as a fundamental
enduring conflict among or between objectives, goals, cus-
toms, plans, activities or stakeholders, which is not likely
to be resolved completely in favor of any polar position in
that conflict. The necessarily temporary resolution of
issues by a public policy is likely over long periods of
times to move closer to favoring one pole over another.
Thus, the crucial question facing public policy in any given
time is striking a fresh balance among conflicting forces.

It is important to distinguish issues from problems.
The solution to a problem is a matter of the application of
knowledge and choice in a definitive way. Problems can be
solved, issues cannot.

In the policy arena there are very few problems.
Consequently, there are few opportunities for solutions and
the search for them is usually sterile. Rather what one
finds is the need to identify alternatives and options, to
identify their consequences and to facilitate the selection
among them.

One characteristic making it difficult to come to grips
with an issue is that any significant public policy matter
is an interlocking and nesting collection of subissues. The
key issue or issues are not obvious, since they usually have
not been presented in a clear, cogent or neutral way by any
of the parties concerned. It is not in their interest to
do so.

Issues are also value-laden. Since values are heterogeneous and overlapping among the parties at interest, it
is difficult to identify and sort them into tidy bundles.
An effective way to reveal the values of the parties to the
conflict is important. That revelation is not likely to
result from simple direct inquiry. The resolution of an
issue in almost all cases must be a compromise rather than
a clear victory for any party to the conflict.

The legislator, regulator, or judge dealing with a
public policy issue rarely finds a clear field, that is a
situation in which much of the underbrush of conflict can
be quickly set aside and definitive action taken. There are
exceptions: first are conditions of crises, which permit
almost instantaneous sorting of the issues and objectives.
The minor issues are submerged and the policy instruments
vigorously played to the clear tune of crisis.

During a perceived civilian crisis, interesting and
sometimes useful action may be taken. For example during
the oil embargo, a nationwide 55 mile an hour speed limit
was imposed--an almost unthinkable action in the course
of normal events. What is interesting about that is not
so much its imposition but the unique opportunity it provided to gather special information which in turn is influencing
a continuation of that regulation.

The policy field is also relatively clear during the
formation of a new agency. The elan, the drive, an openness, a willingness to try to do things as well as a
certain degree of public forgivingness relax some of the
conflict.

This vitality is not likely to be found, however, in
the new agency which is in fact not a new agency but the
product of the reshuffling of the bureaucratic deck. The

formation of the Environmental Protection Agency or the
Energy Research and Development Administration does not
represent a true fresh start on a major problem but a kludge
of mismatched parts, incompatible missions, hold-over staff,
and a residuum of traditional conflicts and biases. The
consequence of such circumstance is often a year or two of
relative paralysis rather than definitive action.

On a larger scale the same applies to a new administration. For reasons mentioned below, those honeymoons are
often brief. What, for example, ever happened to the plans
for the Peace Corps or the Office of Economic Opportunity?

Issues do evolve. Some issues disappear and fresh ones
arise. These patterns may be slow or precipitous. In any
case they largely result from the interplay of evolving and
interacting trends. The trends may be themselves relatively
stable, rising, or descending. Some may even undergo
relatively steep and sudden change. Understanding the interplay of trends is fundamental to understanding both the
origins of issues and their possible evolution. Unfortunately the natural time unit of the evolution of major trends in
society mismatches the time constant of the body politic.
This mismatch is a major reason why issues often are not
effectively engaged.

The world of the elected official, legislator or senior
bureaucrat is an endless roster of major and minor, short and
long term, prominent and subtle problems and issues. A
dominant factor in the selection for attention among these
issues is suggested by an epigram of Al Smith, "the politician's
first obligation is to get elected." Attention is selective-
ly given to those issues that are perceived as most critical
and politically potent among his constituencies. Those
issues are tackled which if ineffectively attended to, are
likely to lead to his loss in the next election or block his
next step up the appointment ladder. Central to the American
system is that the elected official is at greater risk of
losing than he is of benefiting from a big win.   The
result is that the short term and parochial tend to drive out
the long term, the less visible or national matters which
override or contradict the constituents' sharp concerns.
One can take an endless but not a very long trip on this
political-bureaucratic carousel.

Some observations on the nature of social, technological
and political decisionmaking in the United States, particularly from a government point of view, may help set a context
for the analysis and resolution of issues.

FIGURE 1a*

PUBLIC INFORMATION IN THE PRESENT EIS PROCESS

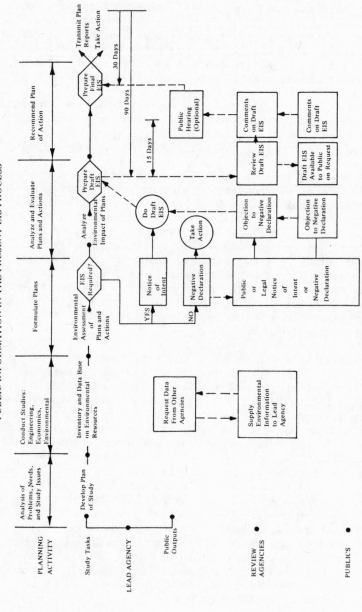

*Environmental Impact Assessment, Edited by Marlan Blisset, Lyndon G. Johnson School of Public Affairs, The University of Texas at Austin, 1975, Chapter 13, p. 221.

FIGURE 1b*

PUBLIC PARTICIPATION IN ENVIRONMENTAL IMPACT ASSESSMENT

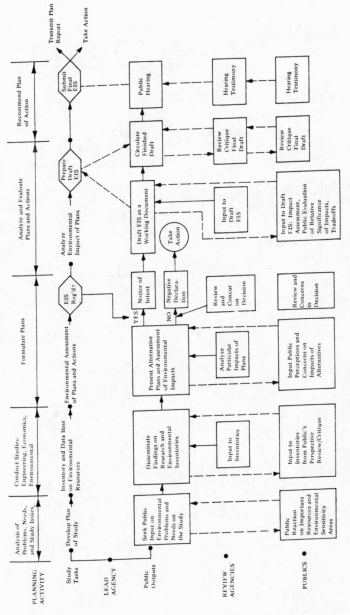

*Environmental Impact Assessment, Edited by Marian Blisset, Lyndon G. Johnson School of Public Affairs, The University of Texas at Austin, 1975, Chapter 13, p. 221.

FIGURE 2*

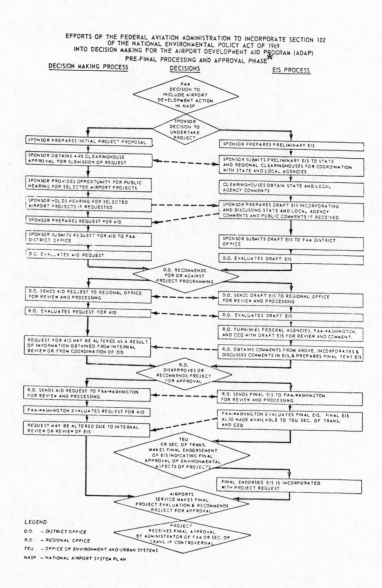

EFFORTS OF THE FEDERAL AVIATION ADMINISTRATION TO INCORPORATE SECTION 102
OF THE NATIONAL ENVIRONMENTAL POLICY ACT OF 1969
INTO DECISION MAKING FOR THE AIRPORT DEVELOPMENT AID PROGRAM (ADAP)
PRE-FINAL PROCESSING AND APPROVAL PHASE*

* U.S. General Accounting Office, Improvements Need in
Federal Efforts to Implement The National Environmental
Policy Act of 1969, Report B170186, May 8, 1962.

o Decisionmaking is disaggregated among at least
  three levels of government and numerous agencies
  at each level. No one has plenipotentiary power.
  While no one person, agency, or institution is in
  charge or has a clear field or the authority to
  accomplish things, often dozens, if not scores,
  of units of government have the power to intervene,
  to slow down, or to stop action by others.

o The complexities of modern government decision-
  making are illustrated in Figures 1 and 2. Figures
  1a and 1b is a generalized diagram of public participation in the environmental impact statement process.
  Figure 2 shows specifics in the process of the EIS
  preparation for one agency, the Federal Aviation
  Administration

o The public policy process of the United States is
  thoroughly adversarial and premised on the parties
  at interest coming forward, in conflict, to express
  their positions or concerns. Two principal difficulties result. Neither separately, nor together,
  do these adversaries or parties at interest adequately map all of the important elements entering into a
  major issue. Their parochialism, however, is not
  just topical, it is temporal. Separately and together
  the parties rarely have more than a myopic time
  horizon. There is no constituency for the future.

o Another fundamental fact of the American political
  situation is that there is no public. There are
  only publics representing partial, factionated,
  astigmatic, myopic, facets of any question. These
  limitations are no less true of the American Banking
  Association, the National Association of Manufacturers,
  the Sierra Club, or Common Cause. It is useless to
  deplore this, but crucial that one understand it and
  take it as basic in engaging a policy matter.

o What follows from this view of forces entering into
  decisionmaking is that the most effective approach
  to the identification and analysis of public policy
  issues is at the intermediate level reflecting the
  limited boundaries of limited authority of any potential user of a study, input, diagnosis, or
  analysis. Against that background policy advice
  that is global in scale, decoupled, remote, or unrelated to the forces on public policy decisionmaking
  in the United States, is beside the point in the
  short run. That is not to say that widesweeping
  analyses do not slowly change the ambience of the

nation, or slowly build new ideological or quasi-
religious movements. But let's not forget that
the cumulative short-term issues in the next twenty
years could kill us all.

o Many issues are not information driven. Yet there
is the frequent desire to bring more information
to bear on an issue. This desire is not only mani-
fest by the parties at interest but also by those
concerned from the inside, the bureaucrat or the
legislator. The search for information is often
a delaying tactic. It can be a mechanism for
apparently taking action while taking no action.
Commissions are perhaps the single most frequent
example of this tactic. Needless to say, it can
backfire since the work of a commission or a study
group may actually shed light on the issue or
build a new constituency on the matter.

Two interesting examples of this are the Marijuana
Commission and the Kerner Commission. In each case,
the Commission came to and campaigned for conclusions
in conflict with the expectations of a large portion
of society and contrary to the albeit vague expectations of the primary client. One commission
concluded that the basic source of riots lay in the
implementation of white prejudice. The other
commission found an allegedly dangerous drug to be
miscategorized, mislabeled and meriting few unequivocal marks against it.

o Public policy decisionmaking is not irrational or
nonrational. Quite the contrary, it assimilates
a wider range of consideration, values and perspectives, under the influence of more hostile,
partisan and vindictive forces than you or I are
familiar with. To deplore or ignore this, to
preach to it or to deny it is at best useless.
The great obstacle for those who would improve the
process is the time and forebearance it takes to
understand it.

o The structural conflict in public policy issues is
most readily visible in Supreme Court cases involving the Bill of Rights. The well-known Miranda Case
involves a conflict between the police powers of the
State and Article of the Bill of Rights which secure
persons, houses, papers and effects against unreasonable search and seizure.

Stating the Issues

Most people operate in ordinary discourse under the general assumption that they understand the issues and that the people with public responsibility also understand the issues. It is important to test that hypothesis. It is my belief that quite to the contrary, even those most intimately associated with issues--public officials, bureaucrats, public interest groups, lobbyists and various stakeholders--often find it to their advantage not to confront the issues, not to define them, not to state them clearly, and not to use them as a basis for discourse, analysis, evaluation and decisionmaking. Take for example any of the current favorite areas of public concern, "oil spills in the Atlantic," "crime in the streets," "housing policy," "energy policy," or whatever, and make the following thought experiment. State the issue as you understand it. The chances are, from my experience, that what you come up with is a phrase, or a question or a platitude. It is unlikely that your issue statement will explicitly be framed in terms of structural conflict. Getting it right is a challenge to one's perspicacity, accuracy, precision, and judgment. It is easier to be vague. Most issues definition is conducted at the level of a teenager, whose favorite recourse in the face of his imprecision and vague understanding is "like, you know."

The statement of the issue can have profound effects on what is done or will be done to clarify and study the matter. Consider, for example, the case of the poor. What is the major national issue of public policy in relation to the poor? The tendency is implicitly, if not explicitly, to interpret the situation into something having to do with jobs, or skills, or information, or nutrition, or education, or discrimination. Rarely does one find such a refreshing address to the problems of the poor as "a lack of money," out of which one can form a variety of alternative public policy issue statements. For example, if the issues of the poor are couched in any of the categories above, major motors of government will move to fill in the educational, nutritional or job skill gap. If however, one suspects that the problem of the poor is the lack of money, one might begin to look, as government recently has, at such things as income maintenance, negative taxes, and so on. Note I have not presented issue statements here, but only talked around them.

Take another area of major public concern--nuclear power. Where does the issue lie in nuclear power? It seems to be a continuing unfolding pattern of new issues over the last twenty years. They have successively related to thermal pollution, nuclear material escapes, safety, meltdown, diversion, sabotage, terrorism, waste disposal, public participation, and information.

There was no conceptual or analytical reason why each of these successive major concerns could not have been identified and thrown into context very early in the development of nuclear power. The reasons are organizational and institutional. It is rarely, if ever, in the interest of the bureaucracy to lay bare its real much less potential difficulties or to probe and question the assumptions underlying its primary concerns. At any given stage in nuclear power development, it would hardly be in the perceived interests of the bureaucracy to open to question its central business, in view of the fact that the system and its leadership almost certainly operate on the notion that in the long pull these vagrant concerns are incidental, trivial, non-existant or overblown and the principal benefits are overwhelmingly desirable and of clear social value. On the other hand, the forces acting to expose difficulties are usually organized along relatively narrow lines and generally have not had the experience or the resources to lay out and analyze the system in its totality. The consequence is infinite incrementalism. Those who are opposed to nuclear power for whatever purpose need at any time only one prevailing objection. As the scale of societal enterprise increases, the investments and commitments become larger and the opportunity costs themselves become tremendous, we need a process to go beyond incremental trouble making, random exposure of deficiencies, dilatory delay and bureaucratic obscuratism and dissimulation. We need a process which in a timely way lays out the difficulties and permits more effectively integrated address to all problems and issues.

The fundamental thesis of this paper is that little public policy analysis goes on framed around issues and there has been relatively little interest by either the user or the producer of such analyses to get on with clarifying the issues.

Another favorite area for issue evasion is crime and delinquency. What are the issues in relation to crime and delinquency? I am sure that you will find the attempt to couch them in conflict terms to be demanding as well as intellectually refreshing. The effort will make clear how alternative statements require different kinds of public policy analysis.

With regard to science and public policy, one finds
issues analysis particularly retrograde. There is little
future oriented applied public policy analysis. Most of it
is historical and explanatory. The social science community
of sociology, political science, psychology and anthropology,
which one might expect to be concerned with public policy
issues, overwhelmingly emphasizes explaining past events,
generating general theories and not bothering to test them,
and examining how the system manages to survive in the face
of all of its difficulties. Much of the policy literature
is the product of senior scientists reflecting their own
limited, albeit important, personal experience and professional biases.

The Role of Government in Public Issues

The future course of every public policy issue of
necessity involves uncertainty. Much uncertainty is not
accidental but intrinsic, and cannot be eliminated for several reasons. First, the future is not fully anticipatable;
second, we do not have adequate models of social change; and
third, many of the consequences of actions associated with
policy cannot be understood until the actions themselves are
taken.

It, therefore, follows that there are several primary
roles of government with regard to public policy issues. A
key role is the provision for the generation, organization,
assimilation, dissemination, and utilization of information
directed at understanding public policy. The melancholy
fact, however, is that there is no adequate much less general
issue-oriented policy information system in any civil agency
of government. Another primary task for government is to
manage uncertainty, i.e., to take those measures which in one
way or another eliminate, hedge, reduce, or compensate for
uncertainty so as to permit the institutions of society to
move ahead in an organized fashion. Events now suggest that
government has been less in the business of managing uncertainty and more in the business of generating and proliferat-
ing uncertainty. A third and major role for government is
the orchestration of the instruments of government to achieve
whatever goals are implied by an analysis of the issues and
the associated policies, programs, and projects initiated
therefrom.

The application of the instruments of government may,
of course, be either directed at threat reduction or the
exploitation of opportunities in the interest of the common-
weal. Unfortunately, the preponderant concerns of government
reflecting the preponderant concerns of thos who are the

active constituents on any particular issue tends to focus more on threat reduction than on new, long-term, different or fresh approaches to bringing great benefits to society. One finds intense discussion about flood plain control, but in fact very little about positive land use planning. One finds much concern about the negative effects on the metropolitan environment of housing subdivisions, highways, and automobile pollution. One finds almost no systematic, effective policies for better cities. Regarding telecommunications there is relatively little serious policy oriented discussions on bringing the great new benefits of telecommunications to the mass of Americans but much to dynamic discussions of threats to privacy and threats to the obsolete concepts of competition.

Tools of Government

If one takes seriously as an overriding principle that public actions should be flexible, foresightful, and embrace feedback, a number of subsidiary points follow. Foremost is that the government cannot do everything. Yet the long-range trend has been to raise more and more public concerns to the national government level and to demand more and more government action on these concerns. This, of course, is part of the cluster of long-term trends associated with the movement of America to a predominately middle-class society. A key social characteristic of the middle class is its reliance less on personal and private provisions and more on institutions—the use of "the system."

The generation of institutions to meet its needs and the agitation against institutions which fail to meet its needs are the order of the day.

A basic conjugate proposition is that government cannot do only one thing. Of necessity, the actions of government have carry-over implications usually unexpected and beyond the bounds of what was anticipated and planned. This lack of surgical precision in government implies that greater attention must be given to the potential implications of government actions before they are taken, and greater attention must be given to monitoring their effects after government acts. To illustrate with one example, the food stamp program is now being used by college students as a form of subsidy. Whether or not this is in the public interest is beside the point. The interesting thing is that it was an anticipatable effect that was not anticipated.

The instruments of government may be directed at individuals such as consumers and individual citizens, or they may be directed at business, industry, and other organizations, or they may be turned back onto government itself.

The instruments of government, while finite and bounded, are nevertheless varied, and numerous. But their potential and actual implementation is rarely orchestrated in a way to meet the three F's criteria above (foresight, feedback, and flexibility). At the highest level of government, the Congress, the principal constitutional functions are budget appropriation, legislation, oversight and investigation, and the setting of public policy. These functions, of course, rarely result in direct government impacts on citizens, but are implemented and activated through the executive branch of the government and reviewed by the judicial branch. The principal tools of government therefore, reside in the executive branch and include as broad categories:

o Information related functions
o Financial incentives and disincentives
o Regulatory and control measures
o Research and development
o Operations
o Policy related activities

Table II suggests some of the diversity of these capabilities in government. When one compares the diversity of tools available to government with the level and sophistication of analyses entering into most policy issues, it becomes obvious that it is unusual for any systematic and comprehensive attempt to be made to integrate, orchestrate, or evaluate the roles of these various tools in achieving public policy objectives. Perhaps more to the point and even rarer are those actions of government which follow through and systematically attempt to monitor the consequences of the implementation of these instruments of government. The net result is that we rarely get early warning of the failures, shortcomings, or successes of the system, but tend to only get signals when catastrophy results.

Some Actors in The Policy Drama

In working out a public policy issue, the principal actors in the drama usually are:

o The decision maker
o The bureaucrat or other users
o The social scientist
o The ideologue
o The publics

TABLE II

INSTRUMENTS OF GOVERNMENT

I. Information Related

o Generation of information by means of
   - data collection, e.g., census surveys
   - demonstration
   - evaluations
   - technology assessment
   - public (e.g., congressional) hearings
   - monitoring
   - research and development on
     a) social cost
     b) public policy alternatives
     c) the system
     d) technology
     e) basic science
     f) intervention experiments

o The packaging of information
   - as by curriculum development
   - definition of costs
   - display of pros and cons

o The dissemination of information in terms of
   - reports
   - seminars
   - extension programs
   - trade fairs
   - conferences, symposia
   - state technical services

o Stimulation of discussion, interest, concern by
   - providing a forum
   - education
   - publicity
   - propaganda
   - lying
   - fear and threats

o Withhold information

o Proposing model legislation

TABLE II (continued)

II. Financial Measures

    o Taxes
      - Residual charges
      - Value added tax
      - Excise tax
      - Income tax
      - Corporate tax
      - Personal tax
      - Customs duty
      - Tax write-offs
      - Tax Deferment or Abatement Subsidies
      - Depreciation and Depletion Allowances

    o Grants

    o Contracts

    o Loans

    o Rewards for innovation and invention

    o Incentives, e.g., matching funds, scholarships,
      loans, grants, forgiveness of loans in return for
      special services, contests

    o Earmarking funds, setting floors and ceilings

    o Insure loans, crops, investments, etc.

    o Compensate for loss

    o Underwrite

    o Set priorities on funding

    o Allocate funds

III. Regulatory and Control Measures

    o Regulate/deregulate

    o Legislate

    o Set standards

    o Certify

o License

o Codes

o Government control or monoply

o Grant rights

o Form interstate compacts or special legal units

o Court Decisions, injunctions, ets.

o Cease and desist orders

o Monopoly privileges

o Inspection requirements

o Fines and punitive damages

o Registration and mandatory reporting

o Audit

o Mandamus

o Substitute criminal for civil sanctions or vice versa

o Institutionalize

o Rationing

o Quotas

o Limit Liability

o Import

o Export

o Copyrights

o Patents

o Prohibitions

o Ban

o Moratoria

o Require warranties

o Zone

o Eminent Domain

o Seize

o Occupy

o Declare Martial Law

IV. <u>Operation</u>

o Building civil works

o Build facilities
  - drug treatment centers
  - sewage disposal plants

o Operate facilities
  - traffic (air and auto) control systems

o Reclaim Land

o Establishment or support of an industrial base
  by government purchase

o Institutionalize, R&D, government departments, semi-
  public corporations, and establishing new institution

o Demonstrate

V. <u>Policy Related Function</u>

o Setting of policy

o Defining priorities

o Set objectives
  - import/export goals

o Delayed decisions

o Coordinate affairs

Let us turn briefly to examine some of the functions, objectives and limitations of each of these actors.

The Decision Makers

It follows from the discussion earlier about the characteristics of decisionmaking in the United States that there are very few decision makers with a broad or exclusive field of responsibility. They often operate in a cluttered field with confused lines of authority. Consequently, if one is attempting to assist the decision maker, it is important to identify who they are and which of them are willing to act on the basis of new information and analysis. This observation is particularly crucial to those outside government who would attempt to render assistance to the decision maker either on a voluntary or a fee-for-service basis. The successful delivery of study inputs to the decision maker depends upon the results being useable within the framework of his authority and responsibility. It does little good to tell the senior police or criminal justice administrator, that crimes are primarily a response to alienation, unemployment, or urban congestion. There may, however, be others for whom such an analysis can be made policy relevant.

In addition to there being few decision makers, most of those who do exist find their principal power is negative. Their ability to stop or to threaten to stop or impede is their most powerful tool.

Most decision makers, particularly those put in office on an elected or political appointment basis, are acutely aware of the likelihood of their terms being brief. Consequently, short-term considerations tend to dominate and to drive out long-term considerations, however important. The short-term turbulence, unrest, and dissatisfaction affect their careers now, whereas the major public payoffs come later when they are likely to have retired, left the job, or moved on to something else.

Recall also that there are almost no protective mechanisms to guard against the negative sanctions so generously and readily heaped on the decision maker. The external forces tend to be a combination of advocacy in favor of parochial interests with powerful negative sanctions in terms of threats and harassment. Incidental to this, it should be noted that as discussed below there are almost no positive feedbacks to provide a reward for effective action anywhere in government.

In supplying public policy analysis on issues to a decision maker who is ready and willing to act on new information, it is important to recognize that three factors are dominant. First, the timeliness of the result. Your work must come in early enough to be related to the decisions to be made. Second, is the quality and even-handedness and balance of the input. Third is the question of credibility. The issue of credibility on the executive side often, but by no means always, is strongly related to the professional and institutional qualifications of the people providing the study. In other words the executive branch can make good use of experts. On the other hand on the legislative side, the credibility criteria are often much broader, demanding inputs and provision for all the parties at interest.

Decisions are made now, hence the bottom line for the decision maker is "what should I do now?" If a decision must be made, even if it is a conservative decision to do nothing, the fact remains that the decision maker must go with what he has. Consequently, those who would assist the decision maker must keep foremost in their mind that the decision must be made now and often cannot be deferred to gather new information, which is not likely to be definitive anyway. On the other hand, one common decision is to defer further decision until more information is at hand.

Many people feel that scientific and technological studies have a great deal to contribute to better public policy. My belief is that those inputs into the decision process will have their principal payoff in a) assisting in the formulation of alternatives, b) the evaluation of alternative actions and their consequences, c) the monitoring and evaluation of outcomes, and d) presenting or balanced even-handed comprehensive analyses.

Bureaucracies
Bureaucrats and Other Users

The fundamental rule of bureaucracy flowing out of the work of Max Weber and numerous analysts since then is that bureaucracies do not exist to perform their primary function. Rather they exist primarily for self-preservation. They tend therefore to be problem and especially issue avoiding.

Bureaucracies in spite of their responsibilities are hardly a source of imagination, ingenuity, drive or openness. The very structure of bureaucracy in cookie cutter categories tends to make it avoid adequately mapping any issue. There

is no payoff and only trouble to be gotten by overstepping
administrative boundaries into the territory of other bureaucracies. Consequently, problems tend to be inadequately
mapped at the level of any bureaucracy. This reflects our
structure of government which is partial, overlapping, and
fractionated. In those rare cases where issues are adequately mapped bureaucracies tend to be hyperconservative and
self-serving of their own interest. After all, anything
new and important can only mean trouble. Furthermore,
bureaucracies are subject to terrible negative sanctions and
have almost no means of enjoying rewards. I know of no
bureaucracy in the Federal government or any bureaucracy in
any state government which has an explicit clear program for
identifying and appropriately rewarding successful performance. Let me suggest as a test question, turn to your
favorate agency and ask what were the 1, 2, or 3 principal
accomplishments of that agency in the past year? Who are
the particular individuals responsible for the accomplishments? Why were they responsible and how were they
identified and rewarded for that responsibility? You will
generally ring up a zilch.

Bureaucracies in dealing with public issues often tend
to avoid issues or to convert them into problems. This
penchant of bureaucracies is reinforced by the kinds of
experts who are drawn upon for advice.

Favorite bureaucratic strategems for avoiding difficulties are to rely on coordination that hinges on an
ambiguity of the term. It can mean either information exchange or the effective integration of programs across
agencies. It rarely means the latter, and it is a protective mechanism to be sure that each agency is taking a
bureaucratically safe action and not infringing on the turf,
the perogatives, or the effectiveness of another agency.

One of the key difficulties in bureaucracy is that there
is little place and almost no protection for the maverick,
for the thinker, for the offbeat, for the dissident, for the
critic, for the innovator.

The ambience of bureaucracy is suggested by the following inscription on wall plaque at a Federal laboratory:

"4 Way Test"

1. Is it the truth?
2. Is it fair to all concerned?
3. Will it build goodwill and better friendships?
4. Will it be beneficial to all concerned?

Bureaucrats and only to a lesser extent legislators and political figures, irrespective of the level of government, have to respond to interest group pressures and to the ineluctable political calendar that cuts their world up into temporal pieces, and which drives towards short-term narrower consideration and gives little affirmative feedback to action directed toward longer term consideration. Remember it's easier to lose than to win. Sanctions outweigh rewards.

From this, it follows that if one is to assist in the identification of issues and their analysis in the service of bureaucracy, one must identify the scope and responsibility of the agency and one must carefully build an understanding of what might be done and bring bureaucrats properly into awareness of those possibilities. One must come up with outcomes which are actionable and in the perceived tangible interest of the bureaucracy. Government is not a religion and bureaucrats are not moral athletes.

The Academic and The Expert

Every society and organization must have a mechanism for coping with trouble. Shamen and priests will undoubtedly continue in this role in every society in one form or another. The expert and the academic fill this functional niche in contemporary society, at least with problems of government and bureaucracy. An expert, whether academy or otherwise, is one who has "acquired special skills in or knowledge of a particular subject." Consequently, the value of the expert is beyond question in dealing with problems. If one has a problem situation, i.e., one for which there is a solution, what better recourse is there to calling upon the expert? Experts have been enormously valuable to government in this regard. The rub comes however, in that many of the most important functions of government, those involving public policy issues, are beyond the competence of expertise. They are not tractable by disciplinary knowledge alone. They are value laden and questions of conflict. Consequently, in calling upon the expert, the bureaucrat or the decision maker is hoping that the expert's specialized but fractionated knowledge can deal with an issue. This is usually a vain hope. One quickly sees that one reaches the limits of where knowledge and authority pure and simple can help clarify the issues. This situation however, is worse than that. It often is in the bureaucrat's interest as a form of shirking responsibility to attempt to convert issues into problems. The expert too, not being expert in conflict, i.e., in public policy issues, tends to want to convert every issue into a set of problems he can treat and let it go at that. One sees, for example, the now conventional examples of this--a highway engineer who ultimately ends up taking the "public be damned" attitude, that is, up to about 1965. One sees this in the military in terms of the tactical expert, who knows how to win battles but has little sense about winning and loosing wars, a political activity.

We must, of course, in this brief essay pass over the question of what and who is an expert, how one identifies them and what is the credibility of an expert? Let us jump right into the problem of the expert in public affairs.

The academic community which is the great promise in the minds of many is so beleagured by a reward system focused on disciplinary performance, the tenure system, good publications, and a system of approbation driving to narrow performance in some technical field, that it is barely able to pull up its socks and deal with any kind of complex public issue in a useful way. This is true whether or not the academic is funded by an agency and whether or not he is working on his own initiative or on a contract. That generalization is not meant in any way to undercut the fact that a tiny percentage of academics in spite of the rewards and sanctions of their system have performed usefully in the public interest. But that is in spite of, not because of the academic arrangements. These few represent unusual rather than common cases. It is important to highlight this sys-temic weakness of the academic community since there is a growing tendency to turn to schools for advice and analysis on public issues. In general the academic is a model of all experts in doing public policy analysis. They run into the following circumscriptions.

o The academic tends to do what he can rather than what he should in dealing with a situation. The political scientist, sociologist, engineer, and economist want to treat the matter at hand in political, sociological, engineering or economic terms. But our world is not built that way. The college catalogue is a poor map of human affairs.

o The academic tends to divide the problem along disciplinary categories rather than treat it holistically. After all, to undertake a holistic treatment of any subject whether it be crime, public transportation, war, or forest management, would require the expert to step outside his expertise and make himself vulnerable personally, psychologically and intellectually. He would have to face matters for which he is untrained.

That learning experience hits very hard at the
ego of a forty-five year old senior professor who
is used to guaranteed accomplishment in a narrow
area sustained and supported by a covey of
graduate students often treating him as a minor
deity.

o If there is a choice about being right, that is,
  impeccable in disciplinary categories, and being
  useful in a sense of public policy conclusions,
  the academic has a strong tendency to opt to be
  right. The result is that the academic whether
  alone or through such institutions as the National
  Academies or academic study teams tends to opt
  for repeating the narrow, the prosaic, the
  certifiable, the pedestrian, and the safe rather
  than engaging the policy issue and going past the
  facts to generate public wisdom. The absolutely
  essential feature of public policy advice is that
  it must go past the facts to point out what it all
  adds up to, to say what makes sense to do. The conflict between being right and being useful is not a
  conflict of right and wrong, but one of vanity and
  self-interest, versus vulnerability and public service.

o There is a tendency to act as if all past knowledge
  of a general or specific sort, in the subject area
  is non-existent; therefore one wants to start from
  scratch. The result is a large allocation of funds
  for repetitive work.

o The academic and the expert has a tendency to be
  cagey with his advice, to be vague, to repeat the
  statement of problem and not to focus on operation-
  ally significant conclusions or recommendations.

o There is a tendency on the part of the academic and
  the expert to ask for more time, more money, more
  effort to study "the problem." The inability to
  achieve closure is probably the single most important liability that the expert and the academic
  brings to public policy issues.

o In general, experts cannot deal with trade-offs
  which are the essense of public policy. Experts
  cannot deal with compromise situations and conflict,
  as experts. That is not to say many haven't become
  successful public policy analysts, but the fact is

the best public policy research is not done in the academic environment, but is done in commercial and non-profit think tanks.

o The problems of the think-tanks, that is, profit or non-profit study groups outside the bureaucracy suffer many of the limitations on the ability to deal with issues that the academic and the bureaucracy themselves suffer. Since most of them operate on a fee-for-service basis and a relatively strict accountability for time, they are often precluded from developing a continuing experience among a cadre of people in policy studies in particular areas. The result is that for many think-tank analysts their work is random, haphazard, ephemeral, high pressured, and time constrained. In addition the recent tendency to put these services on a competitive basis leads to a nearly universal tendency on the part of the think tanks to promise more than they can reasonably deliver. A symbiotic abandonment of common sense by both the client and the sponsor, therefore, leads to study results which are often badly written, poorly thought through and atrociously presented in some bizarre institutional dialect.

o An almost certain condition for successful team treatment of a highly complex interdisciplinary and multidisciplinary issue is the opportunity and the leisure to develop lines of communication among the team members as well as mutual expectations and lines of communications with the clients or the users of the work. Present procurement and business practices virtually preclude that. Successful examples are conspicuous as exceptions not as the mode.

o The bureaucrat and the expert also have a penchant for wanting to convert issues into problems since that provides something he can safely sink his teeth into.

o The successful expert insofar as he has been successful in dealing with problems also suffers the understandable difficulty of wanting to perseverate in those successful strategies. Whether one is an economist, an operations researcher, systems analyst, or engineering designer, success tends to make one want to continue along those same lines. One sees this expert's weakness particularly brought forward in the present tendency of the government to take senior officials from the National Aeronautics and Space Administration and assign them to policy-related responsibilities all over the government.

Usually their first attempt is to "find out what
the problem is." When they discover that the problem doesn't exist, they then proceed to the second
strategy of suboptimization on some problem elements
of the issue. The result is that either no learning
occurs or it takes an extremely long time to recognize that the highly successful and commendable
strategies of the space program are not transferrable
to the civil sector.

One can see this attempt operating in the microcosmic
in such an agency as ERDA in which the general public charge
to promote conservation in energy has been rapidly and effectively converted into a more problem like format of
promoting efficiency in the use of energy. A bit of re-
flection will show that by no means is efficiency congruent
with conservation. But experts sure can spend or absorb
money on that problem.

Efficiency is, of course, one element of conservation
but to limit the concept to efficiency avoids the most
knotty policy issues, creates the illusion of action and
accomplishment while instilling a pernicious degree of
complacency that the matter is being adequately addressed.

The inability to come to grips with public policy
issues is not peculiar to the academic in his academic domain
but tends to be characteristic of any study function heavily
laden with experts and academics, such as the work of the
National Academies of Sciences and Engineering or the work
of various study commissions and such as the Commission on
Violence in Television or the Marijuana Commission.

The Social Scientist as Policy Analyst

An important subset of the academic and the expert
community is the social scientist. He has a superadded set
of difficulties which he tends to bring to policy research.
For this discussion, social scientists would include sociologists, psycholgists, political scientists, and anthro-
plogists, but not the economist, since they are more closely
modeled by the engineer.

Within the social science community, there seem to be
two kinds of tensions which work against effective involvement in public policy analysis. First is the tension between
the quantifiers and methodologists on the one hand and those
oriented toward social concerns. The first tend to be extremely defensive about the scientific components of social

sciences and to my mind are perhaps too fully mimicking some
aspects of the physical sciences. Those emphasizing quantification and methodologies often seem to operate in a most
narrow orbit and have the greatest difficulty in coming to a
sense of public wisdom and advice out of their own work. On
the other hand, those who come from a social work orientation
frequently carry heavy ideological burdens which inhibit
their ability to even entertain, much less conduct, even-
handed, balanced analysis.

The second division among the social scientists which
seems to prevent address to issues is that between macro-
and micro-analysis. Throughout the social sciences--prob-
ably largely a result of the mimicry of the physical
sciences--macro-analysis, dealing with society in the large
in contrast to the specific narrow problems, seems to be in
decline. Yet these are often the areas of public policy in
which social science input would have its greatest value.

As I see it, in general, the social scientist working
on public policy issues can make a minimum but important contribution in providing an alternative perspective or insight. The dilemma is brought out clearly, between the
macro- and micro-thinker if one brings the social scientist
to look at the implications of a strip of highway. The
tendency to focus on the quality of life in the narrow
sense may usefully inform that decision but may entirely by-
pass and overlook the macro-social consequences and might
even lead to a step backward.

A third difficulty with social sciences is that they
seem to be less solution oriented than physical sciences and
engineering.

Another difficulty is that the social scientist is often
speaking a special language which while closely related to
the vernacular, at least superficially, does tend to promote
confusion. Another side of the special language matter is
that simple concepts to the layman often seem to become over
elaborated by social science jargon. So one finds in the
social sciences a particularly crucial need for the art of
plain speaking. Remember, in relation to the discipline
the decision maker is usually a layman.

The Ideologue

Ideologies play a large part in every political system
and in every issues analysis. A particular point to be noted
here with regard to ideologues and public policy analysis
is their desire to convert problems into issues. Frequently

what could be managed at a given bureaucratic level or could
be dealt with effectively by public policy actions becomes
overelaborated by the ideologues. Perhaps the most interesting and systematic example of this is the role of the
American Civil Liberties Union in highlighting first amend-
ment and other threats in virtually every quarter of
government action. By and large, in my judgment, these warnings are justifiable and sound, and merit attention. But the
ideologue's approach is not to look toward solutions of the
problem but to convert them into issues in a mode which fundamentally cannot be dealt with.

An example of this is in the current discussion over
data banks, telecommunications, and privacy. Most of the commercial risks to and violations of privacy are driven by
economic considerations, especially the needs or desires of
creditors, merchandizers, and advertisers. But this clear,
economic drive behind challenges and violations of privacy
has led to almost no serious consideration of economic criteria and solutions to any aspect of the question. It is
for example, feasible to set up price schedules on varying
degrees, or depths of privacy. For those who are less concerned about their records would it be feasible to offer
lower cost goods by permitting various kinds of potential
data uses? On the other hand, those who for any reason are
reluctant to have their data accessible could pay a higher
price for data services. On the other hand, one could consider personal data copyrightable and so subject to fee
collection. I only wish to point out that this kind of
discussion which may offer partial solutions to a network
of problems and issues tends to be driven out of the discussion by the ideologues.

The ideologue also comes in the form of the academic as
macro-thinker. Conspicuous recent examples are the Limits
to Growth, Small is Beautiful, Deschooling of Society. Such
analyses are almost totally decoupled from any mode of action
that any individual bureaucrat, decision maker, or agency can
attempt. Of course, what ultimately does happen is that the
ambience they create becomes watered down, partitioned, and
related to government. But one must be careful not to confuse macro-diagnosis with public policy issues analysis.

Values and Public Participation

Bureaucrats in the last few years seem to have succumbed
to the seduction of two concepts which they perceive respectively as a holy cross protecting them from the devil and the
panacea facilitating all action. The first of these is
"values" and the second is "public participation."

Values

An interesting but yet unexplored historical avenue of
public administration is how the term and concept of values
has so effectively permeated the bureaucracy. When confronted
by a crucial issue or about to engage in a significant discussion, as often as not, the contemporary bureaucrat will
attempt to shunt aside that engagement by saying that it is a
matter of "value judgment." Those two words in juxtaposition
mark the advant garde bureaucratic mentality. Values, of
course, permeate everything and judgment is a primary reason
for which public officials exist. But that two-word phrase
is meant to cast outside the range of bureaucratic responsibility the subject at hand. This is an example of the
proposition mentioned earlier that the bureaucrats want to
convert issues into problems. Consequently, all questions
of value become hallowed and set aside as value-judgments
and hence beyond their concern. One result is that the subject of values has engendered an alarming amount of
intellectual trash, useless discussion,uninformed deliberation, and pointless hand wringing. Another pathological
aspect of considering values, largely resulting from a
professional and upper middle-class orientation toward
thinking, draws from the sound observation that values permeate activities, the false conclusion that making those
values explicit is a worthwhile activity in all public policy
processes.

Those with this middle-class bias tend to ignore the
fact that many private motives are in conflict, are latent,
are dark, uncongenial, and even unspeakable. Consequently,
the universal call for making them explicit and public is
really an invitation to hypocracy. There is a tendency to
misunderstand the role of the elected official and the senior
decision maker in wanting him to make his values explicit.
For him to make his values explicit would be a travesty. The
decision makers role is to adjudicate and to keep his values
internal so he can effectively adjudicate the value-laden
material put forward to him by others.

A characteristic of many of those celebrating the values
discussion is a trained incapacity to use the knowledge that
they have; for example, making the assumption that everyone
is as bright and able as they are. This trained incapacity
is illustrated by:

○   The choice to ignore that many people have
    something useful to say on value-laden

      subjects,

- o Some people's judgments and evaluations are
   better than others, and
- o People can learn by being exposed to good
   thoughful information.

Values are difficult to discern. Individuals often
cannot see their own values. When they can see them, they
cannot give weights to them. Values are often ill-formed.
They are latent, they are dark, they cannot necessarily be
related to public decisions without a great deal of intermediate work. Perhaps, many values are fugitive, shallow,
or in vogue. The key point to note here, however, is the
bureaucratic use of the context of values as a pretext for
failing to tend to business.

Values are best approached in terms of the behavoir of
the value holders. Their past orientation, attitude and
actions reveal values. People are most useful in revealing
values in response to specific analyses, concepts and proposals. In general, any group of laity are at a strong
disadvantage when asked what they think or put in a position
of having to create and generate public policy analysis or
public policy options de novo. They do, however, work
effectively and well in response to material put before them
in a credible feedback soliciting situation. In general,
the search for values and their integration into public policy should not be handled on the model of the search of
spiritual testimony, but rather should be approached as an
empirical matter displaying cognitive and behavioral responses to situations, options and alternatives.

Public Participation

As mentioned earlier, there is no public with regard to
public issues. There are only publics, that is, parties at
interest, collectively, corporately, or individually. Hence
efforts directed at the public at large invariably misfire
and are often if not usually beside the point. The pressures
of public involvement resulting from legal challenge and
legislative mandate have led many agencies to concern public
participation into a kind of a ceremonial unguent which once
applied will facilitate whatever they want to do in the first
place.

The usual bureaucratic effort at participation is pro
forma, stilted, uninforming, non responsive, quasi-legal,
not structured to result in or influence action and not

FIGURE 3

The Policy Research Space

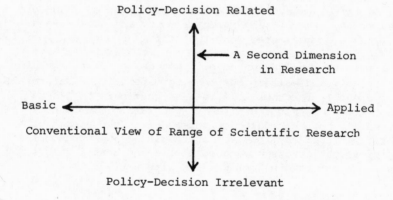

structured to inform decisionmaking. The process of public participation should be one which is continuous, open, informing iterative, responsive, evocative, and tied to decisions. Without going into details of good or bad cases we do seem to be learning to contact if not quite embrace the public.

Applying Contemporary Study
Techniques to Public Policy Issues

This section will highlight a few key considerations in the attempt to apply contemporary analytical tools such as research, study, analysis, modeling, evaluation to public policy issues. Perhaps first to note is that by and large we lack adequate conceptual tools out of the disciplines to engage most of the non-discipline conflict-laden policy issues. Second, most research is disjoint from policy or decisionmaking except in a general way in making an overall contribution to human knowledge. Third, in beginning to move into the application of contemporary tools to policy issues, most initial efforts will be amateurish and inept. One must, therefore, anticipate that many new groups brought into the process will have to enjoy longer time and greater forebearance for their work. As a subsidiary element to that for a number of the reasons described earlier, most otherwise fully competent scientists and thinkers are not particularly cut out for public policy analysis. To the best of my knowledge there is no selection procedure to tell the potentially successful from the unsuccessful candidates for that function.

One must, therefore, be prepared both psychologically and institutionally for a good bit of cut and try. Fourth, most researchers like to think of research as falling along a two-dimensional axis, basic to applied, whereas there is an orthogonal axis of decision relatedness. (See Figure 3.) Many scientists prefer to act as if there is only one axis because the social structure of science puts the prestige at the basic end of that range.

In general, there is no reward structure at all for moving along the policy decision axis. There are sanctions and penalties for stepping outside the disciplinary cocoon, for working with people from other backgrounds and for dealing with the spongey and protean problem of a policy issue. Table III attempts to illustrate examples of this structural conflict to alert the would be policy analyst to the complexities before him.

Table III

Examples of structural elements in conflict on national issues.

Public Policy Issue Areas

1. Legalized Marijuana
2. TV Violence
3. Amnesty
4. Capital Punishment
5. Energy Conservation
6. Urban Redevelopment
7. Nuclear Power Plant Sales Overseas

Structure Elements in Conflict	Short Term Forces	Long Term Forces	National	Regional	Economic	Social	Environmental	Political	Rural	Urban	International	Mil. Nat. Security	Indus'l Bus.	Religion	Civ.Rts Civ.Lib	State/ Local Govern.	Nat'l Gov.
Long Term Forces	2,3,5,6,7																
National	3,5,6	5,6,7															
Regional	3,5,6	5	5,6														
Economic	2,5,6,7	5,6,7,2	5,7,2	6													
Social	3,4,6	3	3	6	2,5,6,7												
Environmental	5	5,6,7	5,6	5,6	2,5,6,7	5,7											
Political	2,3,4,5,6,7	3,5,6,2,7	3,5,7	5,6	2,5,6,7	1,2,3,4,5,6,7	5,7										
Rural	6	5,6	5,6	5,6	5,6	5,6	5	5,7									
Urban	5,6	5	5,6	3,6	5	5	5	5,6	5,6								
International	5,7	5,7	1,7		7	3,7	7	5,7	5,6	7							
Mil. Nat'l Sec	3,5,7	3,5,7	3,5,7		7	3,7	7	7	5		7						
Industr'l Business	2,5,6,7	2,5,7	5,7	5,6	5,6,7	2,5,6,7	5,7	2,5,6,7	5	5,6	7	7					
Religious Moral	7	4,1	4,1			4		7		7	7	7	5				
Civ.Rgts/Civ.Lib	1,2,3,5,6	3,4	6	6	2,4,6	2,4,6		2,4,6	5	5,6	6	7	2,7	4			
State/Local Gov.	5,6	5,6	1,4,7	5,6	2,5	4,5,6,7	5	4,5,6	5	5,6	6	6	2,5,6	2,4	2,4,5		
National Governm't	5,6	3,5,6	4,5,7	5,6	2,5	3,4,5,6,5,7	5	5	5,6	5,6,7	6,7	6,7	2,5,6,7	2,4,7	2,4,5,6	2,4,5,6	1,2,5,6,7

Summary

In summary this paper indicates some of the basic conditions of public policy research and some of the misconceptions or institutional constraints on doing such public service. The paper offers optimistic advice in that the understanding of these conditions and constraints will facilitate useful good work. There are enormous opportunities to benefit the public through the successful address of the policy issues. While you may not know how to do it now, with the proper mind set there is a good chance you can learn and can be effective in working the vague, shifting, uncertain policy terrain. It may, therefore, be appropriate to end this advisory essay to those who would give advice with A Garland of Precepts by Phyllis McGinley:

Though a seeker since my birth.
Here is all I've learned on earth,
This the gist of what I know:
Give advice and buy a foe.
Random truths are all I find
Stuck like burs about my mind.
Salve a blister. Burn a letter.
Do not wash a cashmere sweater.
Tell a tale but seldom twice.
Give a stone before advice.

Pressed for rules and verities,
All I recollect are these:
Feed a cold to starve a fever.
Argue with no true believer.
Think-too-long is never-act.
Scratch a myth and find a fact.
Stitch in time saves twenty stitches.
Give the rich, to please them, riches.
Give to love your hearth and hall.
But do not give advice at all.

NOTE

Several people have usefully commented on earlier drafts of this paper, their successes in my education can be best attributed to their insightful and salient criticism. Their failures are due to my opacity and intransigence.

These benefactors include John Gilmore, Jack Nilles, Dennis Little, Don Kash, Jack White, Dennis Miller, Dorothy Nelkin, Anton Schmalz and Vary Coates.

4

Technology for Director Dubious: Evaluation and Decision in Public Contexts

Ward Edwards

In preparing this paper, I had the enormous advantage of having read the companion paper prepared by Mr. Joseph F. Coates, of the Office of Technology Assessment, U.S. Congress. Mr. Coates's incisive and provocative analysis of the nature of public policy decision making and the difficulties that experts have in providing useful inputs to that process merits extravagant admiration. It is a frank, penetrating review of virtually all of the issues that bemused academics like myself who have fluttered around the fringes of the Federal policy community for many years have vaguely sensed as being characteristic of policy making.

I would like to underline a few points made by Mr. Coates, as a preliminary to some suggestions about what might be done to address them. Perhaps his most important single point is that policy is not made in a problem-oriented vacuum. Instead, it is made in an embattled arena, usually by a man or an organization upon whom are focused the efforts of a wide variety of conflicting stake holders, each having his own perception of both problems and issues—often with his own collection of "facts" to back up that perception. As Mr. Coates says, "The key issue or issues are not obvious, since they usually have not been presented in a clear, cogent, or neutral way by any of the parties concerned. It is not in their interest to do so." In such an embattled context, "The resolution of an issue in almost all cases must be a compromise rather than a clear victory for any party to the conflict." This gladiatorial atmosphere presents problems to the would be policy-influencer, because "In general experts cannot deal with tradeoffs which are the essence of public policy. Experts cannot deal with compromise situations and conflict, as experts."

If one looks for the underlying issues of any conflict, they seem to fall into two categories: probabilities (measures of uncertainty) and utilities (measures of values). Concerning probabilities, Mr. Coates says "The future course of every public policy issue of necessity is involved in uncertainty. Much uncertainty is not accidental but intrinsic, and cannot be eliminated for several reasons. First, the future is not fully anticipatable; second, we do not have adequate models of social change; and third, many of the consequences of actions associated with policy cannot be understood until the actions themselves are taken." I would add that often those consequences cannot be understood even after the actions have been taken. As a result, Mr. Coates says that "Another primary task for government is to manage uncertainty, i.e., to take those measures that in one way or another eliminate, hedge, reduce, or compensate for uncertainty so as to permit the institutions of society to move ahead in an organized fashion." From my own point of view, such measures for uncertainty management have a necessary preliminary: first one must measure uncertainty.

The other issue that Mr. Coates identifies as crucial is the one that he calls value, but I would prefer for history-of-science reasons to call utility. He says, "The subject of values has engendered an alarming amount of intellectual trash, useless discussion, uninformed deliberation, and pointless hand wringing.... Values are difficult to discern. Individuals often cannot see their own; when they can see them, they cannot give weights to them. Values are often ill formed. They are latent, they are dark, they cannot necessarily be related to public decisions without a great deal of intermediate work."

On the question of measuring values, Mr. Coates seems to me to be somewhat ambivalent. At one point he says, "Since values are heterogeneous and overlapping among the parties of interest, it is difficult to identify and sort them into tidy bundles. An effective way to reveal the values of the parties to the conflict is important. That revelation is not likely to result from simple direct inquiry." At another point, he derides"... the false conclusion that making those values explicit is a worthwhile activity in all public policy processes.... Many private motives are in conflict, are latent, are dark, uncongenial, and even unspeakable. Consequently the universal call for making them explicit in public is really an invitation to hypocrisy."

From reading Mr. Coates's paper, one can formulate a picture of two different Federal Government policy-makers, whom I shall call Director Devious and Director Dubious. Mr. Coates describes Director Devious quite well. "The

crucial question facing public policy in any given time is
striking a fresh balance among conflicting forces. . .
The search for information is often a delaying tactic. It
can be a mechanism for apparently taking action while taking
no action. . . Even those most intimately associated with
the issues. . . often find it to their advantage not to confront (them), not to define them, not state them clearly,
and not use them as a basis for discourse, analysis, evaluation, and decision making. . . There is a tendency to
misunderstand the role of the elected official and the senior
decision maker in wanting him to make the values explicit.
For him to make his values explicit would be a travesty.
The decision maker's role is to adjudicate and to keep his
values internal so he can affectively adjudicate the value-
laden material put forward to him by others."

I have much more difficulty in finding in Mr. Coates's
paper a description of Director Dubious. Mr. Coates says
"Government is not a religion and bureaucrats are not moral
athletes." But I believe that, in this as in other areas
of performance, a desire for athletic excellence is built
into many of us, whatever the level of our capabilities for
fulfilling that desire. My image of Director Dubious is
that he is perplexed by the multiplicity of the uncertainties
and the value orientations with which he must cope. While
he recognizes the necessity of functioning as a middle-man
mediating among conflicting stake holders with conflicting
values, in the face of technological and political realities
that are often rather vaguely and uncertainly defined, he
genuinely would like to perform this function as best he
can, and would welcome tools that might help him to do so.
Nor, I think, would he endorse Mr. Coates's advice that he
should keep his own values deeply hidden from others, and
perhaps even from himself. If some of his values are, as
Mr. Coates says, dark, uncongenial, and even unspeakable,
he wishes they weren't. He would like to have some way of
inspecting values, both his own and those of others, and
attempting to make some kind of moral sense out of them in
their relation to the facts of the problem.

If I may lapse for a moment into psychoanalytic jargon,
perhaps Director Devious might be taken as a representation
of the ego of one kind of elected official or senior
decision maker. If so, perhaps Director Dubious is a
representation of the same person's superego.

I feel reasonably confident that Mr. Coates would
regard the tools that I am going to propose for use as
idealistic and naive, and therefore unlikely to be of much
use to a public policy maker. Contexts exist in which I

would agree with him. Nevertheless, each of the two major
tools I plan to discuss is in fact in current use in significant public decision making contexts. Unfortunately, I will
not present examples of the actual application of those tools
to public decisions. For one thing, many of the details of
those applications as they now are in progress are classified
or otherwise confidential. For another thing, even if they
were not, the character of each detailed application is
typically so complicated that any attempt to present the
basic ideas at appropriate length would inevitably fail.
Consequently, I will talk about two relatively simple tools,
both currently in use, in contexts in which they obviously
bear on public policy, and could be used by public policy
makers, but so far have not been.

Evaluating Radiologic Efficacy by Bayesian Methods

My first tool is addressed to the first of the two key
problems that Mr. Coates identified: the problem of uncer-
tainty. The work that I will be reporting comes from the
Efficacy Study of the American College of Radiology, and is
a collaborative effort involving Lee Lusted, Russell Bell,
Harry Roberts, David Wallace, and myself, among a good many
others. The funds supporting it came from the National
Center for Health Services Research of the U.S. Public
Health Service. (For a report on the results so far, see
Lusted, Bell, Edwards, Roberts, and Wallace, in press.)

The essential purpose of the Efficacy Study is to
explore the usefulness of the very large number of X-rays
and other radiologic diagnostic procedures being carried out
in the United States. This particular report is based on
7,976 case studies in various emergency room settings. The
study is ongoing; ultimately, it hopes to explore something
on the order of 60,000 cases in a very wide variety of
settings for radiological practice.

Back in 1971 the American College of Radiology set up
a Committee on Efficacy. Among its motives were a finding
by Bell and Loop (1971) that an X-ray examination of the
skull following a trauma was quite unlikely to show skull
fracture unless certain signs and symptoms were present,
and that the probability was even lower that the radiographic
findings would affect patient management or the final outcome. Bell and Loop estimated that society was paying
$7,650.00 per skull fracture found in patients X-rayed under
those conditions, and they questioned whether the benefits
were worth the cost. More generally, the ACR's Board of
Chancellors had been concerned because the demand for
radiologic services was, and is, growing faster than the

supply, even though costs were also increasing. No rational basis existed at that time, or now, for setting priorities for available radiologic services. Customarily the radiologist performs the radiographic examination that the attending physician requests whether or not the request is appropriate. Although some data do exist suggesting what X-ray examinations are appropriate under what conditions, most radiologists know that on occasion a physician will request a radiologic examination that appears unnecessary and the radiologist receiving the request is likely to meet it.

At its first meeting in 1971, the ACR committee on Efficacy, chaired by Professor Lee Lusted of the University of Chicago, attempted to formulate the problem of what efficacy was and how it might be measured. Three different conceptions of efficacy were proposed, varying both in relevance to the long range problem and in measurability. The most relevant, but also hardest to measure, has come to be called Efficacy-3. Efficacy-3 is long run efficacy from the patient's point of view; that is, a diagnostic procedure is Efficacious-3 if the patient is, in the long run, better off as a result of that procedure and its consequences than he would have been had it not been performed. Obviously, knowledge of long run outcomes is difficult to obtain, and knowledge of hypothetical long run outcomes for sequences of diagnostic and therapeutic procedures other than the one actually carried out is even more difficult to obtain. Consequently, we next considered Efficacy-2. A diagnostic procedure is Efficacious-2 if and only if the course of subsequent therapeutic action taken by the attending physician is different as a result of performance of the procedure than it would have been otherwise.

Obviously Efficacy-2 is easier to measrue than Efficacy-3, since it refers only to events in the immediate future. However, one must still discover what would have been done had constraints existed that did not in fact exist, and that too presents measurement difficulties. So, as a final fallback position, we proposed Efficacy-1. A procedure is Efficacious-1 if and only if the procedure influences the diagnostic thinking of the attending physician. This definition turns out to lead to relatively straightforward measurements. All one must do is to discover what the attending physician was thinking at the time he ordered the X-ray, what he thinks at the time he receives the result, and compare the two; if they are different, the procedure is Efficacious-1, and the size of the difference measures the amount of efficacy.

How does one measure what the attending physician is

thinking? Our procedure was to collect judgments of the
probabilities of possible diagnoses prior to the X-ray, and
another set of judgments posterior to it. Then, by using
Bayes's theorem, one can calculate the extent to which
opinion has been changed as a result of the X-ray. Bayes's
theorem is a trivially simple fact about probability, and
can be represented for our current purposes by the following
equation: LFO = LIO + LLR. In this equation, LIO stands
for Log Initial Odds, LFO stands for Log Final Odds, and LLR
stands for Log Likelihood Ratio. The logarithmic form of
Bayes's theorem is used here in order to make the relationship additive, and in order to make the measure of diagnostic
efficacy, LLR, symmetric around 0. The mathematical details
by means of which this form of Bayes's theorem can be
translated into other forms, and by means of which probability judgments can be related to this equation, can be found
in many places, for example, Edwards, Lindman, and Phillips
(1965).

Obviously, at the time he orders an X-ray an attending
physician may be considering many hypotheses about what is
wrong with the patient. To reduce this large set to a more
manageable set, we chose to define two diagnoses. One of
them was the most important diagnosis, the one that the
attending physician would be most eager not to miss. In the
cases we will be discussing that would be a fracture or some
other medically unpleasant state of affairs. The other
diagnosis was the diagnosis considered most likely; very
often that was "normal".

A pretest of procedures for measuring Efficacy-1 is
reported in Thornburg, Fryback, and Edwards (1975).

Figure 1 shows the front of a typical data collection
form. This was filled out by the attending physician as
a part of the process of ordering an X-ray. Figure 2 shows
the back of that same form, which was filled out by the
same physician when the result of the X-ray was returned
to him. I must emphasize that the attending physicians in
this study were not specially chosen for expertise in
probability. The study was geographically very widely
distributed; radiological settings in emergency rooms all
over the country were used. Radiologists who were willing
to cooperate in the study were brought from those settings
to Chicago where they received roughly two days worth of
training about the nature of the study and about some rather
elementary rules for assessing probabilities. When they
returned to their native heaths, they recruited attending
physicians from among those who frequently requested them
to perform radiological services. They trained the

Patient Name _____   Patient I. D. _____

Date of Birth _____   Sex _____   Case Number _____

AMERICAN COLLEGE OF RADIOLOGY - EFFICACY STUDY: SKULL - EMERGENCY

PART I (TO BE COMPLETED BY CLINICIAN BEFORE RADIOLOGIC PROCEDURE)
(See CLINICIAN'S HANDBOOK for guidance in completing this form.)

A. Clinical Data: For each entry check one box. (Y-Yes, N-No, ?-Equivocal, NA-Not Ascertained)

Y	N	?	ND	WAS REPORTED	Y	N	?	ND	WAS FOUND
				Recent Trauma					Physical Evidence of Injury
				Recent Pain or Headache					Disrupted or Deformed Bone
				Focal Weakness or Numbness					Focal Somatic Neural Defect
				Seizure or Unconsciousness					Bruit or Altered Pulse
				Abnormal Mentation					Abnormal Mentation
				Deafness, Tinnitus, Vertigo					Discolored Eardrum or Otorrhea
				Recent Visual Problems					Eye Signs of Brain Problem
				Defective Speech or Expression					Other Cranial Nerve Dysfunction
				Recent Nausea or Vomiting					Abnormal Tendon Reflex

Other _____   Other _____
(Specify)   (Specify)

B. What is your patient's PROBLEM that causes you to request this examination? _____
_____

C. 1) For the problem in B, state the most important prospective DIAGNOSIS which prompts this
        procedure. _____

    2) What are your odds or probability estimate that the diagnosis in "C-1" will prove correct? _____

D. 1) For the problem in B, state the most likely prospective DIAGNOSIS ("normal" may be used) which
        prompts this procedure (only if different than the diagnosis in C) _____
        _____

    2) What are your odds or probability that the diagnosis in "D-1" will prove correct? _____

E. What is the one major reason for this procedure? (Check one box only)

    [ ] Prove part normal   [ ] Confirm no change   [ ] Institutional policy

    [ ] Confirm diagnosis   [ ] Show change in disease or healing   [ ] Teaching or research

    [ ] Investigate diffuse suspicions [ ] Assess length, position, etc. [ ] Medical-legal

    Other _____

F. Are you presently aware of patient's medical insurance status?

    Not Aware [ ]   Believe patient is: Insured [ ]   Not Insured [ ]

Your Name _____ and/or ACR I.D. Number _____ Date Filled Out _____
(Please Print)

RETURN TO RADIOLOGY AFTER COMPLETING PART II

NOT A PART OF MEDICAL RECORD

Figure 1. Collection Form: Front Side

PART II TO BE COMPLETED BY CLINICIAN AS SOON AS RADIOLOGIC RESULTS ARE KNOWN

G.   Knowing the X-ray findings, now estimate the odds or probability that the:

   1)   "most important" diagnosis stated in "C-1" of Part I is correct _____

   2)   "most likely" diagnosis stated in "D-1", if any, of Part I is correct _____

H.   Enter below any NEW diagnoses based on radiological findings?

   1)   most important new diagnosis _____Code: __ __ . __ __ __)

   2)   most likely new diagnosis (include normal) _____Code: __ __ . __ __ __)

Your Name _____ and/or ACR I.D. Number _____ Date Filled Out _____
        (Please Print)

SIGNIFICANT RADIOLOGIC FINDINGS (To be filled out by radiologist or referring physician):

_____

_____

_____

_____

_____

TO BE COMPLETED BY RADIOLOGY

RADIOLOGIC PROCEDURE CODE: __ __ __ __ __

RADIOLOGIC DIAGNOSES CODES Dx1 __ __ . __ __ __ __ __   Dx2 __ __ . __ __ __ __ __

                          Dx3 __ __ . __ __ __ __ __

SETTING (check one)   ☐ Screening   ☐ Inpatient

                      ☐ Emergency   ☐ Outpatient

RETURN TO Dr. _____ IN RADIOLOGY AFTER COMPLETING PART II

NOT A PART OF MEDICAL RECORD

Figure 2.   Collection Form: Back Side

Table 1

Distribution of Cases Over Procedures

Procedure	Number of Cases
Skull	958
Cervical Spine	862
Chest	2353
Abdomen	839
Intravenous Pyelogram	278
Lumbar Spine	708
Extremities	1878
TOTAL	7876

attending physicians in how to estimate probabilities. Under
the circumstances we have been delighted with the relatively
high quality of the probability estimates that we have
obtained.

The sampling procedure used in this study, like that
used in many other studies of medical practice, has one
overriding principle: those who participated were those who
were willing to participate. We make no apologies for this,
since we know of no very satisfactory way of proceeding
otherwise. Nevertheless, such sampling does present possibilities of bias in generalization to a national population
either of radiologists or of attending physicians. Consequently, pending the outcome of further detailed analyses
we are performing to explore the possibility of sample bias,
generalizations from our results to such national populations
should be done with extreme caution and nontrivial amounts
of skepticism.

Various procedures explained in detail in Lusted et al.
(in press) were used to spread cases widely over 47 different
emergency rooms and about the same number of radiologists,
between large and small hospitals, between teaching and
non-teaching hospitals, and over a wide variety and number
of attending physicians.

As of July, 1976, the data base was distributed over
X-ray procedures as is shown in Table 1.

As usual in any kind of statistical study, there are
technical problems, and I must discuss one: the truncation
effect. Some respondents responded in probabilities and
some responded in odds, but either way most of them worked
with relatively small numbers of discrete levels of the
quantities they were estimating. In the middle range of
uncertainty, this hardly matters, but the extreme ends of
the scale required particular attention. The problem is
more severe for clinicians who reported in probabilities.
Many of these, in spite of emphatic attempts to train them
otherwise, made estimates of 0 or 1; both of those numbers
are uninterpretable in Bayesian arithmetic. We adopted an
editing convention of calling 0, .0001 and calling 1, .9999.
These rounding conventions, combined with the fact that
most attending physicians responded in probabilities and
used only discrete sets of numbers, produced rather peculiar
structures in the analyzed data. Figure 3 presents a
scatter plot of log likelihood ratio against log initial
odds over all procedures. You can see several parallelogram
patterns that correspond to different common truncation
limits used by groups of attending physicians, or imposed

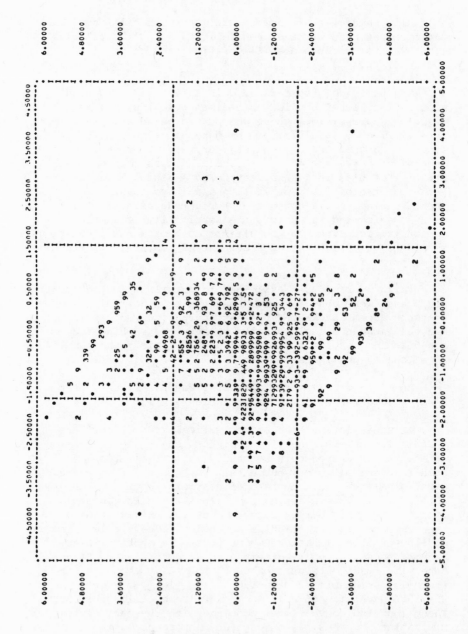

Figure 3. Log likelihood ratio as a function of log initial odds.
Physician responses in 4005 cases for all seven
radiologic diagnostic procedures.

by us since we could not work with estimates of 0 or 1. We
have, of course, devised methods of analysis that are insensitive to what happens at the extremes of the probability
scale. For a more detailed discussion of this technical
topic, see Lusted et al. (in press).

Although the study is far from complete, it is possible
to base some reasonably convincing conclusions on the data
so far. First, the procedure is feasible; that is, such
probabilistic assessments can be made in an orderly way
and do provide information about the diagnostic thinking of
attending physicians. We base this conclusion less on data
analysis than on informal contact with the physicians who in
fact made the assessments.

Our second conclusion is that the impact of X-ray examinations on diagnostic thinking was evident in the vast majority of cases and was substantial in most. Overall, not
more than 10% of examinations seemingly had no influence on
diagnostic thinking (that is, produced a 0 log likelihood
ratio). A more detailed and refined analysis of the data
suggest that the actual percentage of 0-information X-rays
may be less than 5%.

Our third conclusion is that at the time X-rays were
requested, the requesting physician was normally uncertain
about the correctness of his tentative diagnosis. About 4
times in 5, however, the probability of the tentative most
important diagnosis was assessed at less than 1/2; over
half the time, it was assessed at less than about .15. In
other words, the most important diagnosis often had the
character of a not-very-likely medical disaster.

Our fourth conclusion is that about 3/4 of the examinations produced a lowering of the clinician's initial probabilities for the tentataive most important diagnosis. In
other words, on the whole, the effect of radiology in the
emergency room setting tends to be one of reassurance rather
than one of confirming alarm. This conclusion has implications for the relationship between Efficacy-1, diagnostic
efficacy, and Efficacy-2, treatment efficacy. Reassurance
is clearly just as appropriate, from the point of view of
Efficacy-1, as would be confirmation of one's worst fears.
On the other hand, it seems quite likely that this finding
might imply that X-ray procedures that are highly Effica-
cious-1 may not be especially Efficacious-2. We propose to
attack that question in later studies, if we succeed in
establishing that our current rather tentative ideas about
how to measure Efficacy-2 are in fact workable.

Table 2

Percentage of Cases with Log Odds
Less than -1.75 or Greater than +1.75

Procedure	Before Radiography	After Radiography	Net Increase
Skull	15.9	69.9	54.0
Cervical Spine	20.8	77.4	56.6
Intravenous Pyelogram	6.1	54.7	48.6
Lumbar Spine	15.8	74.2	58.4
Chest	8.4	55.0	46.6
Abdomen	5.9	45.7	39.8
Extremities	8.4	75.8	67.4
All Procedures (7876 cases)	11.0	65.0	54.0

Our fifth conclusion is that the major effect of X-rays is to reduce uncertainty. This was no surprise. Even after examination, however, nearly 40% of clinicians assess probabilities for the most important tentative diagnosis at more than .02 but less than .98. This suggests that a substantial fraction of diagnostic decisions in the emergency room setting are based on weight of evidence rather than proof beyond reasonable doubt. Table 2 shows for various X-ray procedures the percentage of cases with log odds that are either less than -1.75 or greater than +1.75. Those numbers correspond to probabilities of .02 and .98 respectively.

An interesting sixth conclusion, at least from the study so far, is that the influence of X-ray examinations on diagnostic thinking was broadly similar for interns, resident physicians in training, and practicing physicians. Also other characteristics, such as the distribution of initial probabilities for diagnoses and the use of odds or probabilities in the expression of uncertainty, were similar for the three groups.

Some other conclusions can be reached from the data, particularly having to do with the question of how well attending physicians used the probabilities they estimated to express their uncertainty. Since these are highly technical in character, I will not review them. I will only add that in general, attending physicians tend to overassess the probability of the relatively unlikely medical disasters that were usually taken as most important diagnoses. Exactly the same kind of finding, of overassessment of the probability of highly undesirable events, has occurred in a number of other contexts in which probability estimators have the opportunity to confuse their judgment of probability with their assessments of the value of the consequence of the event whose probability was being judged. (See Kelly and Peterson, 1971)

A final implication of the study may surprise some. One of the questions asked on the initial form was whether or not the X-ray study was being performed for medical-legal reasons. This box was sometimes checked and sometimes not. Though minor differences between the results when it was checked and when it was not did occur, we were quite surprised at how small they were. In general, X-rays taken for medical-legal reasons are fully as Efficacious-1 as X-rays for which the attending physician does not indicate that he has such reasons in mind.

How does this study bear on public policy? At the moment, it has no direct bearing. It does suggest that the

methodology used is in fact useable, and yields significant
information about the behavior of the individuals performing
socially important and policy-relevant functions. It is
conceivable that refinements of the same methods, combined
with methods for measuring Efficacy-2 and perhaps even
Efficacy-3, might lead to policy-relevant recommendations
about the conditions under which it is or is not most advis-
able to recommend that X-rays be taken. If such a happy
result were to occur, the potential for improving the distribution of health care services might be significant.

Beyond that, however, there is a much more general implication of the study. It shows that decision makers, in
this case attending physicians, can and will, with a little
training and encouragement, make probability assessments
concerning the issues with respect to which they are making
decisions. Since uncertainty enters into every decision and
probability is the appropriate metric by means of which to
quantify uncertainties, this means that the hope of assessing the probabilities that enter into decisions affecting
public policy may not be a vain one.

I need not rest this assertion solely on this particular study. Many other decision makers besides physicians
must deal with uncertainty, and are in process of finding
the explicit use of probabilities a helpful tool for
doing so. We are all acquainted with the fact that probabilistic weather forecasting is coming to be more and more
widely performed. (See for example Murphy and Winkler,
1974.) Even more interesting, at least to me, is the growth
in use of explicit probabilities among public officials
responsible for providing informational input to decision
makers concerned with vast issues of global public policy.
For public discussions of relevant technology, see Edwards,
Phillips, Hays, and Goodman (1968), Kelly and Peterson (1971),
Barclay and Randall (1975).

In sum, then, Director Dubious, eager to come to terms
not only with his own uncertainties but with the uncertainties of those who advise or attempt to influence him, has
available to him a quite elaborate technology, based on
explicit assessment of probabilities. That technology is
already in use, and its generality and simplicity invites
optimists like me to suppose that that use may extend and
spread into other contexts. Perhaps Director Dubious can be
helped to become at least somewhat less dubious about uncertainties.

Multiattribute Utility Measurement as a Tool for
the Explication and Aggregation of Social Values

As I read Mr. Coates's discussion of the latent, dark uncongenial, and even unspeakable nature of private motives, I was quite unclear whether he considered this to be desirable, deplorable, or simply a fact of life. But since I don't believe Mr. Coates's premise about the unattractive character of private motives, whether that premise is desirable or deplorable seems to be beside the point. Most motives, public or private, are mundane, ordinary, and reasonably well organized toward the problem at hand. My own motives in deciding what to include in this paper, for example are to present two intellectual tools that I think may be useful to public decision makers in as effective a light as I can manage, and in the process to be entertaining and perhaps to get a gentle argument going with Mr. Coates. Behind those surface motives, I may well have better-concealed motives to the effect that if the technologies that I am advocating are in fact perceived as useful, I may gain in prestige, in research funding, in opportunities for consultancies, and the like. None of these motives seem too latent, dark, or uncongenial; and I can guarantee that they are not unspeakable, since I just spoke (or at any rate wrote) about them. Many, perhaps most, of the motives that affect ordinary executives in their working lives have essentially this character.

Mr. Coates made eloquent reference in his paper to the two real problems about motives. One is that different people, and especially different pressure groups, have different motives, whereas the decision maker must make a decision that is responsive both to wishes of those whom he serves and to the technological facts of his problem. The other is that any single person's motives, whether private or public and whether latent or explicit, are virtually always in conflict. And, of course, every public policy decision requires value tradeoffs. In order to do better with respect to some dimensions of value, we must do worse with respect to others. But what are the appropriate exchange rates?

A new technology of value tradeoffs has been developing very rapidly over the course of the last nine years. It is called multiattribute utility measurement, and it is particularly prominent in the writings of Howard Raiffa, Ralph Keeney, R.A. Howard, and myself. Relevant references include Raiffa (1969), Keeney and Raiffa (1976), Howard (1973), and Edwards (1977, in press).

The essential idea of multiattribute utility measurement is that every significant value can in effect be partitioned into a set of sub-values on each of a number of dimensions. Technological devices exist for ascertaining what those dimensions are, for locating each one of the actions, objects, or whatever is being evaluated on each of these dimensions for judging how important each dimension is to the aggregate value of the thing being evaluated, and then for performing the aggregation. Details of this technology vary substantially from one of its advocates to another, but the description as I have just given it would probably be agreed to by all.

As in the case of probabilities, I intend to review an application that has potential public policy relevance rather than an application in being. There are in fact several applications already in being, and they have been described in open literature. However they are quite complicated. Two examples are: Chinnis, Kelly, Minckler, and O'Connor (1976); and O'Connor, Reese, and Allen (1976). See also Edwards, Guttentag, and Snapper (1975), and Keeney and Raiffa (1976). The particular application that I intend to discuss is to the selection of nuclear waste disposal sites. The work was performed in collaboration with Dr. Harry J. Otway, who is Director of the Research Project on Technological Risk Assessment, sponsored by the International Atomic Energy Authority and the International Institute for Applied Systems Analysis. For a more complete report of this study, see Otway and Edwards (in press).

Otway's project has two main goals. One is to measure the attitudes of various publics toward the risks associated with various modern technologies in general, and with nuclear power production technology in particular. The other is to explore methods by means of which the technological decision makers who must manage nuclear power activities can be aided in taking public attitudes into account in their decisions. This particular study was addressed to the latter question. The study was conducted during the course of an international meeting of high level technologists concerned with the problem of nuclear waste disposal. The ten participants included representatives from eight countries with advanced nuclear energy programs. Since the conference was in part about problems of risk assessment and risk management in nuclear waste disposal, they were very much concerned with the problem and very cooperative. Otway planned the study, enlisted the cooperation of the respondents, and collected the data. I did not attend the meeting.

The first task, of course, was to find what dimensions
of value were relevant to the problem of selecting waste
disposal sites. Since Otway's goal was to demonstrate how
to take social attitudes toward those sites into account in
the decision process, obviously social attitudes had to be
one such value dimension, and indeed it was the first one
listed.

Elicitation of value dimensions was done by simply ask-
ing all the respondents, together in a room, to identify
what issues seemed to them important in making such decisions. Table 3 shows value dimensions and measures for six
sites. After Otway had suggested social attitudes as the
first such dimension, there was some question about how such
attitudes should be scaled, and it was agreed that for the
purpose of this demonstration a simple 0 to 100 scale would
be appropriate with 100 as a highly favorable attitude and
0 as a highly unfavorable one.

The next dimension, proposed by one of the participants, was remoteness of the waste disposal site from a population center, measured in km. 160 km. was considered as
having a value of 100 and 0 km. was considered as having a
value of 0. The third dimension was the geospheric path
length in km. Roughly, that is the distance a radioactive particle must travel, typically through the ground,
to reach the nearest point used by people. Again 160 km.
scores 100 and 0 km. scores 0. The fourth dimension was
proximity of the waste disposal site to natural resources
such as mines. 160 km. scores 100, 0 km. scores 0. The
fifth dimension was geological disturbance probability--
the probability of one or more significant-sized earthquakes in a year. 10^{-6} (one chance in a million) scores 100
and 1 scores 0. The sixth dimension was the relative migra-
tion rate of the critical nuclide, in the geological formation, allowing for adsorption and desorption, compared with
the rate of movement of ground water (assumed constant at
0.3_5 m/day). Since this dimension is a ratio, it has no units;
10^{-5} was scored as 100 and 1 was scored as 0. The seventh
dimension, elicited from the respondents only after a great
deal of struggle and effort, was transportation distance
between the nuclear plant and the waste disposal site. Zero
km. scores 100 and 1.600 km. scores 0.

Note that all dimensions are transformed onto the 0
to 100 scale in such a fashion that higher scores are pre-
ferable to lower ones. The scaling of the dimensions was
chosen in such a way that the respondents seemed likely to be

Table 3

Descriptions of Six Hypothetical Nuclear Waste Disposal Sites

Value Dimension, Range, and Scaling	Site 1	Site 2	Site 3	Site 4	Site 5	Site 6
D1. Public attitude. 0 = extremely negative; 100= extremely positive	40	20	10	40	60	70
D2. Remoteness from population center, km (90 km = 0; 160 km = 100)	40	12	12	120	40	120
D3. Geospheric path length, km (0 km = 0; 160 km = 100)	40	12	12	4	4	40
D4. Proximity to natural resources, km (0 km = 0; 160 km = 100)	50	150	150	50	15	15
D5. Geologic disturbance probability per year (1 = 0; 10^{-6} = 100; linear in exponent)	10^{-4}	10^{-5}	10^{-4}	10^{-6}	10^{-5}	10^{-6}
D6. Relative migration rate of critical nuclide (1=0; 10^{-5} = 100; linear in exponent)	10^{-3}	10^{-3}	10^{-2}	10^{-1}	10^{-2}	10^{-1}
D7. Transportation distance, km (1600 km = 0; 0 km = 100)	1500	500	500	1500	150	150

willing to treat the single dimension utilities as linear
with the physical measures involved--and indeed they were.
In the case of dimension 5 and dimension 6 this linearity is,
of course, with the exponent rather than with the number
itself.

In retrospect, several features of the scaling of the
dimensions were questionable. The most obvious is the use
of 1 as the highest probability of an earthquake in a year.
No one would seriously propose a nuclear waste disposal site
with so high a probability of an earthquake; a lower probability should have been used as the upper bound.

It is important to emphasize that all sites were assumed to have the same biological characteristics, and that
use of any of them was assumed to fall within appropriate
budget constraints.

The value model to be used in this particular exercise
was a simple weighted average model. Such value models are
quite common, and have been exposed to a great deal of
criticism by decision analysts (e.g. Keeney and Raiffa, 1976)
who complain, quite correctly, that they do not capture sub-
leties in the value structure that people may bring to a
problem. Those, like myself, who like to use simple structures, and who feel that the simplicity of eliciting numbers
built around those structures is more important than getting
the model structure just right at the cost of enormously en-
hanced complexity of elicitation technique, are happy that
a number of approximation theorems show that value structures elicited in this way will, under conditions such as
prevailed in this experiment, often be very close approxi-
mations to much more elaborate and sophisticated value
structures that would have required very much more difficult,
complicated and socially unacceptable judgments. (See
Yntema and Torgerson, 1961; Dawes and Corrigan, 1974,
Wainer, 1976; and von Winterfeldt and Edwards, 1973(a), 1973
(b).)

In order to perform a simple evaluation of this kind,
the next necessary step is to obtain the weights that are to
be associated with the various dimensions. My preferred procedure for doing this is to ask each respondent, working
separately, first to rank the dimensions in order of importance, from most to least important. Then he arbitrarily
assigns an importance weight of 10 to the least important
dimension, and then moves up through the dimensions making
ratio judgments about the relative importances of each of
the more important dimensions compared with the least important dimension. Since he can also make ratio judgments of
the various dimensions to one another, he can obtain a great

many internal consistency checks to make sure that he is in
fact not unduly succumbing to whole number tendencies or any
of the other vices to which this kind of judgmental procedure is subject. This was done for each respondent.

Finally, in order to see whether the apparatus that
thus had been developed for assessing the attractiveness of
waste disposal sites was appealing to the respondents, it
was necessary actually to consider some waste disposal
sites. So far, the entire process had been carried out
without reference to any specific site. However, a number
of sites that have been proposed as possible ones for nuclear
waste disposal were used as the basis for judgment on the
seven relevant dimensions, and the result is shown in Table
3. The ranges of the various dimensions that were actually
encountered in the sites were much smaller than the ranges
that had been anticipated as possible; this fact has
important methodological consequences which I will discuss
in a moment.

So far as the respondents were concerned, the final
procedure was to ask them to make holistic evaluations,
which means ratings on a 0 to 100 scale, of each site, for
comparison with the multiattribute utility evaluations.

Otway asked each respondent to judge the importance
weights of the seven value dimensions twice and consequently
we could calculate test-retest reliabilities of these judgments. Correlations between first and second judgments were
very high; the mean was .93. For convenience, all subsequent calculations used the second set of weights. The
interrespondent agreement about importance weights was, as
you would expect, much lower. Correlations among second
judgment weights between pairs of respondents range from
+.97 to -.27, with a mean of +.39. Actually, this is a
somewhat higher level of inter-judge agreement than has
been found in some other applications of this particular
technique (e.g. the OCD example in Edwards, Guttentag, and
Snapper, 1975). I have argued elsewhere (Edwards, 1971,
in press; Edwards, Guttentag and Snapper, 1975) that individual differences in values should show up primarily in
assessments of the importance of value dimensions. Single-
dimension utilities are often technical judgments rather
than value judgments.

Obviously, the question that would be of primary
interest to Mr. Coates, and also to me, is: How do we go
about reducing, removing or otherwise dealing with these
individual differences in values?

At this point, unfortunately, time pressure problems arose. The best way to do it would be to normalize the importance weights for each individual separately, to average them, to calculate the ratios of importance weights specified by the averages, and then to feed those ratios back to the judges, sitting as a group, and ask them to debate them until they reach some form of agreement about a final set of such judgments that they were willing to allow to be used in a decision process. We did indeed normalize and average, but Otway could not feed back and reconcile differences. In a different context, I have tried this process of feeding back and reconciling differences, with quite good results. (See Edwards, in press.) And I would anticipate that some procedure of that sort would be the essential ingredient in any large-scale application of this technology to decisions over which there are major social conflicts. In the contexts in which the technology has so far been applied, however, the issues involved have been so profoundly technological that such a procedure has not generally been used. Instead, the experts on each of the kinds of numbers were asked to reach consensus about the numbers within the field of their expertise, and were usually able to do so quite well. Perhaps this technology is more easily applicable to fields in which this kind of technological resolution of conflict is appropriate than it is to contexts involving broader kinds of social conflicts.

Now we must turn our attention to the range problem that I mentioned earlier. Consider, for example, dimension 3, geospheric path length. Its actual range covers only 22.5% of the range that originally had been assigned to it. This can easily happen in situations, such as this one, in which the evaluation scheme is developed before the entities to be evaluated are known. Yet exactly that must often be done.

The reason why this presents a problem is that the range of utility values of a value dimension is in a sense a kind of importance weight. A dimension whose utility values range from 0 to 50 is effectively only half as important in controlling evaluation as one having the same weight whose utility values range from 0 to 100.

This problem can be solved only by judgmental methods. However, some mathematical techniques exist that help to put it into perspective. It is possible to transform both of the single-dimension utility values and the importance weights in such a fashion as to preserve unchanged the preference ordering over the options and the utility spacing

Dimensions	Sites					
	S1	S2	S3	S4	S5	S6
Public attitude	50	16.7	0	50	83.3	100
Remoteness from population center	25.9	0	0	100	25.9	100
Geospheric path length	100	22.2	22.2	0	0	100
Proximity to natural resources	25.9	100	100	25.9	0	0
Geologic disturbance probability per year	0	50	0	100	50	100
Relative migration rate of critical nuclide	100	100	50	0	50	0
Transportation distance	0	74.1	74.1	0	100	100
Aggregate utility $(\Sigma_i w_i u_{ij})$	45.6	57.3	40.4	38.2	41.0	57.9

Table 4

Rescaled single-dimension utilities and aggregate utilities
at six nuclear waste disposal sites

between options, while putting all of the single-dimension
utility functions on a scale whose minimum in fact falls at
0 and whose maximum in fact falls at 100. Table 4 shows the
result of doing so. Inspection of that table will show
that no one could possibly pick site 3. In technical jargon, site 2 dominates site 3; that is, site 2 is at least
as good as site 3 on every dimension, and definitely better
on at least one. No other site is dominated. Also note
that site 6, although evaluated as best by the weighted
utility criterion, does not dominate site 3; site 3 is better
than site 6 on the dimensions of proximity to natural resources and transportation distance.

The transformations which I have discussed permit ex-
ploration of the extent to which the scaling of the single
dimension utility functions influences the ultimate outcome.
I won't go into the details, but I can say that in this
particular instance, which is rather extreme in deviations
of the actual from the anticipated ranges, the effect on
preference orderings was extremely modest. In other words,
this procedure is rather robust to errors of anticipation
of that sort.

Finally, consider the relation between the holistic
ratings for the other sites by the respondents and the multiattribute utility ratings. The mean correlation in holistic
ratings between pairs of correspondents is +.20, and the
range is from +.97 to -.55. Note that the respondents
are even less in agreement about holistic ratings than they
were about importance weights. That too is a common finding
in applications of this method. The correlation between
mean holistic ratings and multiattribute utility ratings is
+.58. Both procedures consider site 6 to be best and site
3 to be worst. This correlation between multiattribute
utilities and holistic ratings is somewhat high compared
with most other such correlations in the multiattribute
utility literature, although it still shows that the two
procedures do lead to different results. That on the whole
is gratifying. After all, there would be no point in procedures like multiattribute utility measurement if direct
numerical assessments produced exactly the same results.

Except for various technical details having to do with
intercorrelations among dimensions, both in value and in
physical characteristics, and with the effect of these on
scaling procedures, that's the end of the story of this
particular study, except for one important addition. Harry
Otway informs me that the respondents thoroughly enjoyed the
study, found the importance weights that they had judged

extremely enlightening, and requested him to be prepared to repeat the study at their next meeting, with a considerably more realistic setting and paying considerably more attention to the details of how the study is done.

As I have said before, much more sophisticated and complicated versions of exactly the same technology have been used and are now being used to make major socially important decisions. Several have been published in unclassified sources. For example, one (Chinnis et al, 1976) has to do with the selection of the winning bidder from among a number of bids in a very large-scale procurement of an important and expensive item of military hardware. The additional complexities of the method were concerned primarily with the much larger number of dimensions that were taken into account, the use of a hierarchical value model rather than the simple value model I have presented here, and the introduction of scenarios and scenario probabilities as a tool for the assessment of values. While these technological details are all of fundamental importance to real applications, nothing in them changes the basic idea I have presented in this rather simple-minded exposition.

Nor are all the examples military. In one published application, (Edwards, Guttentag, and Snapper, 1975) a technique of essentially this character was used to help a major agency within the Department of Health, Education, and Welfare to make decisions about the allocation of its research budget for a year. In another application, now in progress, the same kind of technology is being used in planning the rate at which a government agency should encourage a boom town to boom. Still another application now in progress is to the National Program for Decriminalization of Status Offenders. A great deal of data has been collected by Professor Solomon Kobrin and his collaborators at the Social Science Research Institute of USC on the impact of this program both on the juveniles with whom it deals and on the criminal justice and related agencies who must deal with these juveniles. We are now collecting multiattribute utility measurements from a number of experts on juvenile delinquency, crime, the juvenile justice system, and the like, and expect to use these judgments in the process of assessing what the overall effects of this major national program in fact have been, and whether those effects are good or bad, and how good or how bad.

Conclusion

This paper, after some initial questioning of the assertion that major issues of public policy are inaccessible to technological tools, has attempted to illustrate the nature of two technological tools, and to suggest how they can be and are being used in the course of making major social policy decisions. Obviously, I would not want to claim that these tools are optimal, that they are fully developed, or that they should be used for all such decisions. Their applicability is quite limited, as I have attempted to suggest in the course of sketching their nature. Within that area of applicability, however, I believe that they can help those charged with responsibility for social policy in dealing with the two key problems that Mr. Coates identified: uncertainty, and difficulties in assessing and reconciling values.

As Mr. Coates correctly pointed out, no technological tool is likely to be of very great use to Director Devious. His conception of his function, and his goal structure, makes him essentially uninfluenceable by the technology of decision making. Indeed, only the part of that technology that has to do with budgeting and the assessment of costs is likely to get very much of his attention.

On the other hand, as I suggested at the beginning of this paper, Director Dubious is less impervious, mostly because he is less convinced that social policy making must continue to be done in the way in which it always has been done. I conceive of Director Dubious as a skeptical but open-minded man, interested in technological innovation and willing to explore the possibility that a particular technological innovation may have something useful to offer him. I have suggested two possible candidate technologies for his attention.

References

Barclay, S. & Randall, L. S.   Interactive decision analysis aids for intelligence analysts. Technical Report DT/TR 75-4. McLean, Va.: Decisions and Designs, Inc., December, 1975.

Bell, R. S., & Loop, J. W. The utility and futility of radiographic skull examination for trauma. New England Journal of Medicine, 1971, 284, 236-239.

Chinnis, J. O., Kelly, C. W., III, Minckler, R. D., & O'Connor, M. F. Single channel ground and airborne radio system (SINCGARS) evaluation model. Technical Report DT/TR 75-2. McLean Va.: Decisions and Designs, Inc., August, 1976.

Coates, J. F. What is a public policy issue? Unpublished manuscript.

Edwards, W., Lindman, H., & Phillips, L. D. Emerging technologies for making decisions. In New directions in psychology II. New York: Holt, Rinehart, and Winston, 1965.

Edwards, W., Phillips, L. D., Hays, W. L., & Goodman, B. C. Probabilistic information processing systems: Design and evaluation. IEEE Transactions on Systems Science and Cybernetics, 1968, SSC-4, 248-265.

Howard, R. A. Decision analysis in systems engineering. In Miles, R. F., Jr., (Ed.), Systems concepts. New York: Wiley, 1973.

Keeney, R. L., & Raiffa, H. Decisions with multiple objectives: Preferences and value tradeoffs. New York: Wiley, 1976.

Kelly, C. W. III, & Peterson, C. R. Probability estimates and probabilistic procedures in current-intelligence analysis. IBM Rep. 71-5047. Gaithersburg, Md.: International Business Machines, 1971.

Lusted, L. D., Bell, R. S., Edwards, W., Roberts, H. V., & Wallace, D. L. Evaluating the efficacy of radiologic procedures by Bayesian Methods: A progress report. In Snapper, K. (Ed.), Models and metrics for decision makers. Washington, D. C.: Information Resources Press, in press.

Murphy, A. H., & Winkler, R. L. Probability forecasts: A
    Survey of national weather service forecasters.
    Bulletin of the American Meteorological Society, 1974,
    55, 1449-1453.

O'Connor M. F., Reese, T. R., & Allen, J. J. A multi-
    attribute utility approach for evaluating alternative
    Naval aviation plans. Technical Report DT/TR 76-16.
    McLean, Va.: Decisions and Designs, Inc., September,
    1976.

Otway, H. J., & Edwards, W. Application of a simple multi-
    attribute rating technique to evaluation of nuclear
    waste disposal sites: A demonstration. Vienna,
    Austria: International Atomic Energy Authority, in
    Press.

Raiffa, H. Preferences for multiattributed alternatives.
    RM-5868-DOT/RC. Santa Monica, CA: The Rand Corpora-
    tion, 1969.

Thornbury, J. R., Fryback, D. G., & Edwards, W. Likeli-
    hood ratios as a measure of the diagnostic usefulness
    of the excretory urogram information. Radiology, 1975,
    114, 561-565.

von Winterfeldt, D., & Edwards, W. Costs and payoffs in
    perceptual research. University of Michigan, Engineer-
    ing Psychology Laboratory Report 011313-1-T, October,
    1973. (a)

von Winterfeldt, D., & Edwards, W. Flat maxima in linear
    optimization models. University of Michigan, Engineer-
    ing Psychology Laboratory Report 011313-4-T, November,
    1973. (b)

Wainer, H. Estimating coefficients in linear models: It
    don't make no nevermind. Psychological Bulletin, 1976,
    83, 213-217.

Yntema , D. B., & Torgerson, W. S. Man-computer cooperation
    in decisions requiring common sense. IRE Transactions
    on Human Factors in Electronics, 1961, HFE-2, 20-26.

5

Judgment, Choice
and Societal Risk Taking

Paul Slovic

Citizens of modern industrial societies are presently
learning a harsh and discomforting lesson--that the benefits
from technology must be paid for not only with money, but
with environmental degradation, illness, injury and premature
loss of life. Although people have some control over the
level of technological risk to which they are exposed,
reduction of risk typically entails increased expense,
reduced freedom or effectiveness, or other reductions of
benefit, thus posing serious dilemmas for society.

The urgent need to help society cope with problems of
risk is forcing the development of a new intellectual
discipline, "Risk Assessment." The scope and pervasiveness
of problems of risk requires an extraordinary degree of
cooperative effort on the part of specialists from many
fields. Technical issues, such as the identification of
hazards and the measurement of their probabilities and
consequences, require the efforts of physical scientists,
biological scientists, and engineers. Social issues,
pertaining to the importance attached to risks by society,
involve lawyers, political scientists, geographers,
sociologists, economists and psychologists. Specialists in
decision making attempt to coordinate this diverse expertise
and organize it in a manner conducive to improved decisions.

My talk today will address the social aspect of risk
assessment--in particular I shall examine the determinants
of perceived and acceptable risk.

In examining this topic, I am knowingly committing one
of the sins for which Reverend Coates, in his chapter, has
rightfully admonished academics. Rather than treat the
question holistically, my limitations force me to analyze
it from a narrow perspective, that of a cognitive
psychologist. At some time in the future, perhaps, some new

breed of scientist will come along and put all the cognitive, social, economic, and political ingredients together in a form maximally useful to the policy maker. All I can attempt today, however, is to describe the recent efforts of a rather small group of psychologists who are trying to translate knowledge about the workings of individual human minds into information that might help people and society cope more effectively with risk.

Coping Intellectually with Risk and Uncertainty

The first point that I would like to stress is that those who promote and regulate high risk technologies need to understand the ways in which people think about risk and uncertainty. Without such understanding, well-intended policies may not achieve their goals, or worse, may backfire. Although research on this topic has been greatly neglected, there is a small body of knowledge that I believe is policy relevant. My goal today is to outline some of the basic conclusions of this research.

Perhaps the most important general question that the cognitive psychologist could address is whether or not human beings are intelligent enough to deal effectively with risk. Let's examine this question.

Decisions about societal risks require high-level thinking and reasoning on the part of both experts and the public. They require an appreciation of the probabilistic nature of the world and the ability to think intelligently about low-probability (but high-consequence) events. As Alvin Weinberg (1), writing about the problems of nuclear power, noted, ". . . we certainly accept on faith that our human intellect is capable of dealing with this new source of energy" (p. 21). But are we justified in placing such faith in the ability of the human intellect to cope effectively with risk? Although the intellectual capacity of human beings has traditionally been held in high esteem, the faith of those of us who study human decision processes has been shaken.

Probabilistic Thinking

Consider, for example, probabilistic thinking. Because of its importance to decision making, a great deal of recent effort has been devoted to understanding how people perceive and process the probabilities of uncertain events. By and large, this research indicates that intelligent people systematically violate the principles of rational decision making when judging probabilities, making predictions, or

otherwise attempting to cope with probabilistic tasks.
Frequently, these violations can be traced to the use of
judgmental heuristics, mental strategies whereby people try
to reduce difficult tasks to simpler judgments (2). These
heuristics may be valid in some circumstances, but in others,
they lead to biases that are large, persistent, and serious
in their implications for decision making.

Availability Bias

This is not the place to pursue a full discussion of
heuristics and biases in probabilistic thinking. Extensive
reviews are available in the literature (3). However, one
heuristic bears mention here because of its special relevance to public perception and acceptability of risk. This
is the "availability heuristic" whereby an event is judged
likely or frequent if it is easy to imagine or recall
relevant instances of that event. In reality, instances of
frequent events are typically easier to recall than instances
of less frequent events, and likely occurrences are easier to
imagine than unlikely ones. Thus availability is often an
appropriate cue for judging frequency and probability.
However, since availability is also affected by numerous
factors unrelated to likelihood, reliance on it may lead to
overestimation of probabilities for recent, vivid, emotion-
ally salient, or otherwise memorable or imaginable events.

The notion of availability is potentially one of the
most important ideas for helping us understand the distor-
tions that occur in our perceptions of low-probability,
high-consequence risks. For example, the availability
heuristic implies that any factor that makes a hazard highly
memorable or imaginable—such as a recent disaster or a
vivid film (e.g., "Jaws")—could seriously distort the
perceived risk of that hazard.

Sarah Lichtenstein, Baruch Fischhoff, and I have
recently collected data on perceived frequency of various
causes of death that shows the biasing effects of availability (4). We found that the frequencies of dramatic
causes of death such as accidents, homicide, cancer,
botulism, and tornadoes, all of which get heavy media
coverage, were greatly overestimated. Asthma, emphysema,
and diabetes were among the causes of death whose frequencies
were greatly underestimated. These diseases are relatively
common in their non-fatal form and deaths are rarely
attributed to them by the media. In addition to
demonstrating availability bias, this study indicates
that otherwise intelligent individuals may not have valid

perceptions about the frequency of hazardous events to which they are exposed. That, I propose, is a policy relevant conclusion.

Desire for Certainty

Next, I'd like to discuss another aspect of intellectual deficiency. Implementing any new technology is a gamble of sorts and, like other gambles, its attractiveness depends on the probabilities and magnitudes of various gains and losses. Yet scientific experiments (5) and casual observation show that people have great difficulty making decisions even about very simple gambles whose probabilities and payoffs they know precisely.

The risk-benefit conflicts starkly posed by gambles trigger anxiety. One way to counter this anxiety is to deny the uncertainty, to deny that life is a gamble, to view the world as perfectly safe--or at least safe enough so that you don't need to worry about the risk. This happens often with regard to natural hazards such as earthquakes and floods. Thus many of the flood plain residents studied by Kates (6) flatly denied the possibility that floods would ever recur in their areas. Some thought that new dams in the area made them 100 percent safe. Others attributed previous floods to a freak combination of circumstances unlikely ever to recur. Denial is also observed in insurance decision making where people often treat low probability hazards as if they were completely impossible (7). With nuclear power, the opposite reaction occurs; its risks are seen by some as so great that the decision to stop its development is easily made.

When scientists explicitly point out the gambles involved in societal risk taking, decision makers and the public become upset. Borch (8) noted the annoyance of businessmen who receive probability distributions from their consultants when what they really want to know is _exactly_ what the outcome of their decision will be. Just prior to hearing a "blue ribbon" panel of scientists report being 95% certain that cyclamates do not cause cancer, Food and Drug Administration Commissioner Alexander M. Schmidt said, "I'm looking for a clean bill of health, not a wishy-washy, iffy answer on cyclamates" (9). Recently, Senator Muskie called for "one-armed" scientists, who do not respond "on the one hand, the evidence is so, but on the other hand. . . ." when asked about the health effects of pollutants (10). A few months ago, when people all over the country were demanding to know whether or not the swine flu vaccine was safe, the nature of their demands suggests that they were really trying to determine whether or not it was _perfectly_ safe.

Perseverence of Beliefs

The difficulties of facing life as a gamble contribute
to the polarization of opinion about technologies such as
nuclear power or genetic recombination; some view these
technologies as extraordinarily safe while others view them
as catastrophes in the making. We could take some comfort
in the possibility that these polarized beliefs would be
responsive to evidence. Unfortunately, even this solace is
denied us by research showing the extraordinary perseverence
of prior beliefs in the face of contradictory evidence (11).
Once formed, initial impressions structure and distort the
processes through which subsequent evidence is interpreted.
The reliability and validity of new evidence is determined
by its consistency with the prior belief. Contradictory
evidence tends to be dismissed as unreliable, erroneous, and
unrepresentative. Thus, one's opinions tend to be invulner-
able to challenges posed by new bits of information
confirming an opposing view or discrediting one's own
beliefs. Ross (12) concluded a review of this phenomenon as
follows:

> To change impressions, theories, or data processing
> strategies, therefore, it requires more than
> exposure to a fair or unbiased sample of new
> evidence. It is not contended, of course, that
> new evidence can never produce change--only that
> new evidence will produce less change than would
> be demanded by any logical or rational information-
> processing model. Thus, new evidence that is
> strongly and consistently contrary to one's
> impressions or theories can and frequently does
> produce change--albeit at a slower rate than would
> result from an unbiased or dispassionate view of
> the evidence (p. 51).

Comment

More could be said about maladaptive mental tendencies
(e.g., people's misperceptions of causation in probabilistic
environments, which leads them to equate good decisions with
good outcomes and bad decisions with bad outcomes; biases of
hindsight which make people believe, after the fact, that
they knew all along what would happen, etc.), but I think,
the point is clear. In case I have given the impression
that only the public has problems, I should like to balance
the slate. Many of the difficulties and biases have been
shown as well in the judgments of experts (13).

Sinsheimer (14) argues that the human brain has evolved to cope with certain very real and concrete problems in the immediate, external world and thus lacks the proper framework with which to encompass many conceptual phenomena. People have faced decisions of great consequence, like those involving technology, only within their recent history. Following Sinsheimer's reasoning, it might be argued that we have not had enough opportunity to evolve an intellect capable of dealing conceptually with uncertainty. We are essentially trial-and-error learners, in an age where errors are becoming increasingly costly.

Determinants of Acceptable Societal Risks

Next I'd like to discuss some preliminary research on the determinants of acceptable societal risks. When "weighing the benefits against the risks" of technology, the ultimate question policy makers must answer is: "Is this technology acceptably safe?" Or, alternatively, "How safe is safe enough?"

We need to develop a model of risk acceptance that would be useful to systems designers and policy makers. Such a model should not dictate what risks society should accept but, instead, should reflect the public's considered values and preferences.

There are several basic ways to determine the social values that should comprise a model of acceptable risk. Two methods that I'd like to discuss today are based on what are known as revealed and expressed preferences.

Revealed preferences. The revealed preference method advocated by Chauncey Starr (15) assumes that, by trial and error, society has arrived at a nearly optimal balance between the risks and benefits associated with any activity. Therefore, one may use economic risk and benefit data to reveal patterns of acceptable risk-benefit tradeoffs. Acceptable risk for a new technology would be the level of safety associated with ongoing activities having similar benefit to society. Starr derived what may be regarded as "laws of acceptable risk" from this approach. These included (1) the acceptability of risk is proportional to the magnitude of the benefits derived from the activity in question, and (2) the public is willing to accept much greater risks from voluntary activities (e.g., skiing) than it would tolerate from involuntary activities (e.g., food preservatives) that provide the same level of benefit.

Thus we see that Starr's model has two basic components,

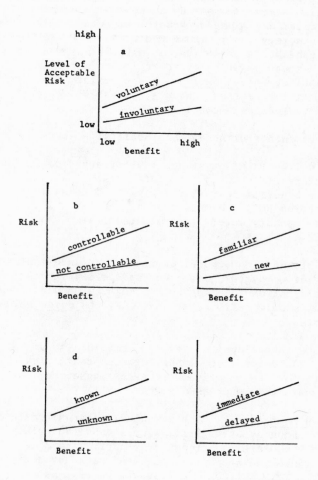

Figure 1
Determinants of acceptable risk as indicated
by revealed and expressed preferences. Adapted from
Starr (1969) and Fischhoff, Slovic, Lichtenstein,
Read & Combs (1976).

benefit and voluntariness, as schematized in Figure 1a.

The method of revealed preferences is attractive because it is grounded in the possible (i.e., in reality); it apparently reflects stable relationships; and it incorporates in some way the impacts of a wide range of economic factors (not just those known by the participant in an expressed preference survey). However, it has several drawbacks; it assumes that past behavior is a valid predictor of present preferences, in a world where values may change quite rapidly; politically, it is quite conservative in that it enshrines current economic and social arrangements; it assumes that what has been traditionally acceptable is also best for society; it makes strong (and not always supported) assumptions about the rationality of people's decision making; it may be unresponsive to particular kinds of risks, like those with a long lead time (e.g., most carcinogens) with regard to which the market responds sluggishly; finally, it is far from trivial to develop the measures of risks and benefits that are needed for its implementation (16).

Expressed preferences. The most straightforward method for determining what people find acceptable is to ask them to express their preferences directly. The appeal of the expressed preference method is obvious. It elicits current preferences, thus being responsive to changing values. It also allows for widespread citizen involvement in decision making and thus should be politically acceptable. It has, however, some possible drawbacks which seem to have greatly restricted its use. Among them are: people may not really know what they want; their attitudes and behavior may be inconsistent; different ways of phrasing the same question may elicit different preferences; values may change so rapidly as to make systematic planning impossible; people may not understand how their preferences will translate into policy; and people may want things that are unobtainable in reality.

At Decision Research, my colleagues and I have recently used the method of expressed preferences to replicate and extend Starr's work (17). In this study, we asked people to rate either the total risk or the total benefit accruing to society from each of thirty activities and technologies. We found that people believed that more beneficial activities should have higher risk levels, and, that a double standard existed for voluntariness, as in Figure 1(a). However, we also found that other characteristics of risk, such as the degree to which the risk seems controllable, familiar, known, and immediate also induced double standards, as schematized in Figures 1b - 1e. The results indicated that the degree to which an activity's risk was potentially catastrophic, dread, and likely to be fatal (given a mishap) also influenced acceptability. Thus, this study implies that a method of determining acceptable risk may need to give weight to all of these various characteristics. Consideration of these characteristics also made acceptability of a risk highly predictable. Conceivably policy makers might be able to use such information to predict public acceptance of the risk levels associated with proposed technologies.

Understanding and Forecasting Public
Response Towards Nuclear Power

I have presented the above material regarding general intellectual predispositions and specific attitudes towards risks under the presumption that it is relevant for policy making. In this section I'd like to illustrate its relevance by applying it to questions about the present and future public response towards nuclear power. Obviously, since the research I've been describing is in its early stages, what follows should be viewed as speculation.

At present, the nuclear industry is foundering on the shoals of adverse public opinion. A tenacious and sizable opposition movement exists. Some nuclear plants have been cancelled. Many others have experienced costly delays. Any attempt to plan the role of nuclear power in America's energy future must consider the determinants and possible future course of this opposition.

Why is Nuclear Power Presently Unpopular?

While the determinants of public opposition are undoubtedly complex, the psychometric survey data obtained by Fischhoff, et al. (17), give some clues as to why nuclear power is meeting such great opposition. For one, its benefits appear unappreciated, being lower, in this study, than those of home appliances, bicycles, and general aviation. Perhaps this is because nuclear power is seen merely as a supplement to other sources of energy, which themselves are viewed as adequate. Second, its risks are seen as extremely high. Only automobile accidents, which take about 50,000 lives each year, are viewed as comparably risky. Third, the acceptable level of risk is judged to be quite low. Our subjects wanted nuclear power to be far safer than they now perceived it to be.

Why are Nuclear Power Risks So Frightening?

Nuclear power is frightening because it has the dubious

distinction of scoring high on many characteristics that heighten anxiety and stimulate aversion to risk. Fischhoff, et al., found that its risks are seen as involuntary, delayed, unknown to those exposed or to science, uncontrollable, unfamiliar, potentially catastrophic, and severe (certain to be fatal). Nuclear power is also perceived far higher on the characteristic "dread" than any of the 29 other items studied by Fischhoff, et al. This may stem from its association with nuclear weapons (the Hiroshima syndrome) and from fear of radiation's invisible, permanent bodily contamination that manifests itself in terms of genetic damage and cancer (18).

Nuclear power risks are also highly "available" (e.g., imaginable, memorable) because of their association with nuclear war and because their dread character leads to extensive media coverage which keeps them in the public eye. As Zebroski (19) noted, "fear sells"--the media dwell on potential catastrophe--not on the successful day to day operations of a power plant.

Will Nuclear Power Ever Be Acceptable to the Public?

On the basis of the research described above, I would speculate that any degree of acceptance of nuclear power could occur, ranging from vehement public opposition, sufficient to topple a government, to rather placid acceptance of the sort now bestowed upon X-rays and dams.

Extreme public rejection is likely to originate from nuclear power's high-risk characteristics as discussed above. This rejection, once aroused, is likely to persist for several reasons. First, the low probability of nuclear mishaps makes demonstration of nuclear safety difficult from a statistical standpoint. Any mishap will be seen as proof of high risk but proof of high reliability would take a massive amount of evidence (20). Second, as noted above, new evidence is likely to be distorted to confirm prior beliefs rather than modify them. Thus, for example, intense effort to reduce nuclear risks may be interpreted by opponents to mean the risks are great rather than that the technologists are responsive to the public's concerns. Likewise, minor mishaps are viewed by those with anti-nuclear predispostions as near catastrophes and knowledgable opinions of experts who rebut such claims may be discounted on the grounds that their close association to the mishap implies that they have some vested interest in minimizing it. Nelkin's (21) case history of debate during a nuclear siting controversy illustrates the inability of technical arguments to change opinions. She found that information available on both sides of the

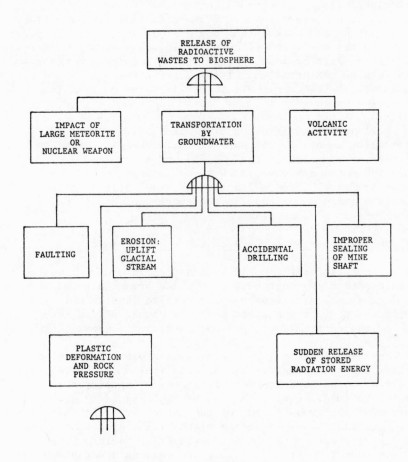

Figure 2
Fault Tree of Salt Mine used for Storage of Radioactive Wastes
(after closure of the mine). From P. E. McGrath,
U.S.-EURATOM Report EURFNR-1204, 1974.

controversy tended to reinforce the conflicting value
positions by highlighting technical areas of ambiguity.
Citizen groups used the debate mainly to legitimize their own
positions.

Availability bias poses a further barrier to open,
objective discussions of nuclear safety. Imagine an engineer
explaining the basis for the estimated safety of disposing
nuclear wastes in a salt mine by outlining the fault tree
upon which the estimate was based (see Figure 2). Rather
than reassuring the audience, such a presentation might have
the opposite effect ("I didn't realize there were that many
things that could go wrong"). Thus I would speculate that
availability effects might make it difficult to engage in
objective attempts at discussing low probability hazards
without, at the same time, increasing the perceived probability of those hazards. Anecdotal confirmation of this
speculation comes from one frustrated nuclear proponent who
lamented, "When laymen discuss what might happen, they sometimes don't even bother to include the 'might'" (22).

With all this working against it, how could nuclear
power gain acceptance? One path requires a long-term safety
record so outstanding it cannot be denied, the development of
respect and trust towards the responsible institutions, and,
of course, clear appreciation of benefit. The risk-benefit
relationships shown in Figure 1 suggest that a quicker path
to acceptance might be forged by a severe energy shortage
resulting in brownouts, rationing, or worse, thus enhancing
the perceived benefits from nuclear power and (as the studies
above suggest) increasing society's tolerance of its risks.
A recent example of this is the oil crisis of 1973-74 which
broke the resistance to offshore drilling, the Alaskan pipe-
line, and shale oil development, all of which had been
delayed because of their threat to the environment.

All in all, public acceptance of nuclear power appears
likely to be precarious, subject to great fluctuations with
the tide of events.

Conclusion

The study of human cognitive processes indicates that
making decisions about risky activities is difficult and we,
as individuals, may not be well equipped for the task. This
leads me to the critical question: "What are the implications of human intellectual deficiencies for societal risk
taking?"

From this follows a number of sub-questions: Can

society rise above the limitations of individual minds? Are new technologies forcing us to make decisions that we cannot make well (or successfully)? Should we take smaller steps in our technological development, so that we can recover from the inevitable mistakes? What kind of political institutions are needed to preserve democratic freedoms and insure public participation for problems involving extreme technical complexity, catastrophic risk, and great uncertainty? If public debates and communications from experts do little to allay fears and, indeed, may exacerbate them, how should we structure public participation? What role can education play in helping society understand and cope with risk?

Although the study of individual human minds is a rather narrow starting point for examining societal risk taking, it appears to lead quickly to important issues that need to be addressed by the entire community of scientists, policy makers, and public citizens.

References and Notes

1. A. M. Weinberg, Amer. Sci., 64, 16, 1976.
2. A.Tversky & D. Kahneman, Science, 185, 1124, 1974.
3. P. Slovic, H. Kunreuther & G. F. White, in Natural Hazards: Local, National and Global, G. F. White, Ed. (Oxford Univ., New York, 1974); P. Slovic, B. Fischhoff & S. Lichtenstein, in Ann. Rev. Psychology, 1977; A. Tversky & D. Kahneman, op. cit.
4. S. Lichtenstein, P. Slovic, B. Fischhoff, B. Combs, & M. Layman, Dec. Res. Rep. 76-2, Eugene, Ore., 1976.
5. S. Lichtenstein & P. Slovic, J. Exp. Psychology, 101, 16, 1973.
6. R. W. Kates, Dept. Geography, Paper 78, Univ. of Chicago, 1962.
7. P. Slovic, B. Fischhoff, S. Lichtenstein, B. Corrigan & B. Combs, Dec. Res. Rep. 76-6, 1976; H. Kunreuther, R. Ginsberg, L. Miller, P. Sagi, P. Slovic, B. Borkin & N. Katz, Limited Knowledge and Insurance Protection: Implications for Natural Hazard Policy (Wiley, New York, 1977).
8. K. Borch, The Economics of Uncertainty (Princeton Univ. Press, Princeton, N. J., 1968).
9. Eugene Register Guard, 1976.
10. E. E. David, Science, 189, 891, 1975.
11. L. Ross, unpublished ms., Stanford Univ., 1976.
12. Ibid.
13. P. Slovic, B. Fischhoff & S. Lichtenstein, op. cit.
14. R. F. Sinsheimer, Amer. Sci., 59, 20, 1971.
15. C. Starr, Science, 165, 1232, 1969.
16. H. J. Otway & J. J. Cohen, Res. Memo. 75-5, IIASA,

Laxenburg, Austria, 1975.
17. B. Fischhoff, P. Slovic, S. Lichtenstein, S. Read & B. Combs, <u>Dec</u>. <u>Res</u>. <u>Rep</u>. 76-1, Eugene, Ore., 1976.
18. R. J. Lifton, <u>Bull</u>. <u>Atomic</u> <u>Sci</u>., <u>32</u>, 16, 1976.
19. E. L. Zebroski, in <u>Risk-benefit Methodology and Applica-tion: Some Papers Presented at the Engineering Foundation Workshop</u>, D. Okrent, Ed. (<u>Rep</u>. <u>ENG-7598</u>, UCLA, 1975).
20. A. E. Green & A. J. Bourne, <u>Reliability Technology</u> (Wiley, New York, 1972).
21. D. Nelkin, <u>Bull</u>. <u>Atomic</u> <u>Sci</u>., <u>30</u>, 29, 1974.
22. B. L. Cohen, <u>Bull</u>. <u>Atomic</u> <u>Sci</u>., <u>30</u>, 25, 1974.
23. I am indebted to Sarah Lichtenstein and Baruch Fischhoff who have collaborated with me on much of the research described in this paper.

6

Observations on Judgment and Public Policy Decisions

Kenneth E. Boulding

Economists look at things rather differently from psychologists, although it is fundamentally the same landscape at which we look. It always amuses me, for instance, that what an economist calls "equilibrium," that is, the highest point of the possibility fence on the utility surface, psychologists call "frustration." This no doubt is because economic man has perfect mental health. Economists look at the decision process as involving, first, a set of alternative images of possible futures in the mind of the decision-maker (the agenda). Then there must be an evaluative process which orders these images in order of "goodness" and the decision is simply to move into the most highly valued image of the future. This is what we call "maximizing behavior" and it is of course only a truism, although, if something is known about the structure and determinants of agendas and the evaluation process, something can be said about it. Thus, decisions involve both agendas and judgment, that is, evaluations, and can be altered either by change in the agendas themselves or in the evaluation process which ranks them.

A simple form of evaluation is where the image of the future can be described in terms of certain quantities for various dates and then each quantity multiplied by some valuation coefficient or "shadow price," as an economist would call it, which converts it into a quantity of some measure of value. Then these quantities or measures of value are simply added up. The process of valuation is certainly more complex than this. The valuation coefficients themselves are functions of the quantities in the agenda, and there may be a kind of gestalt process by which different images of the future are ranked, so that we may derive our valuation coefficients as much from the complex process of evaluation as we derive our values from the valuation coefficients. Valuation coefficients also are variable. They tend to fol-

low a generalized law of diminishing marginal utility, which
is that the valuation coefficient tends to decline the larger the quantity of the thing which is being valued. Valuation coefficients may become negative, of course, in which
case the things valued are "bads" rather than goods. Almost
any particular item tends to be a good in small quantities
and a bad in large.

A very interesting question is whether there is a theory of bad decisions. It is not easy to define a bad decision, but we are pretty sure that some are worse than others.
One definition is in terms of regret, but this of course is
always in terms of hindsight, and it is hard to minimize
regret at the time we make the decision. The principle is
not meaningless and leads into certain decisional rules.
The question of whose regret is also important. I may
regret somebody else's decisions and not have much power to
alter them.

The all too pervasive uncertainty of the future and the
large random element in all social processes makes the evaluation even of past decisions difficult. The question is:
How do we tell good luck from good management? The answer
presumably is: Only by observing over a long enough period
so that probabilities become frequencies. My old teacher,
F. H. Knight, made a very fundamental distinction between
risk and uncertainty, risk being where we know the probability and hence the event is intrinsically insurable, and
uncertainty, where we cannot know the probability simply
because there is not a large enough universe. All we can
have is subjective hunches. The critical question is whether recording and analyzing the results of past decisions
will improve decision-making in the future and, if so, what
structures and processes will produce this effect? I wish
I knew the answer to this question. Bad decisions can arise
out of false agendas, that is, unrealistic images of the
future, which are derived either from poor records of the
past or from "superstitions," that is, the perception of
regularities which do not in fact exist. The social sciences should be able to produce better information about the
past and should be able to reduce superstition, but much
research indicates, as Dr. Slovic suggests, that strongly
held superstitions are remarkably hard to budge, and that in
the presence of uncertainty they are easily confirmed.

What we are really talking about in this session is
"assessment," which is something that should go far beyond
technology. Indeed, I don't really know what technology
has done to deserve so much assessment when other things do
not get assessed. Assessment is essentially evaluation of

decisions and strategies, institutions and organizations, in
terms of human betterment according to somebody's evaluation
or according to some process of coordinating individual
evaluations. All values that we know about are human values,
although more primitive processes of evaluation do exist in
lower animals, and even in a sense in chemical valency. A
study of these evaluations by the method and ethic of science I have been calling "normative science." Evaluations
take place at many levels. We have, for instance, accounting evaluations--the "bottom line" of a profit and loss
statement. This represents essentially the gross increase
in net worth of a complex aggregate of economic goods,
reduced to money values by valuation coefficients which are
loosely related to the set of market prices. We are constantly performing social evaluations, as for instance when
a department selects one candidate as a colleague and
rejects another, when we elect one president and reject
another. Here we come out with rank orderings rather than
with cardinal numbers, but the impact is much the same. It
is only rank orderings indeed that determine decisions; cardinal numbers are merely a crutch to assist us in the process of ranking. One suspects that ranking is all that matters in the real world and that cardinal numbers are a com-
fortable figment of the human imagination, a sort of security blanket of scientism.

Any kind of overall assessment involves some process of
coordination of the diverse evaluations of different individuals. Even though evaluation only goes on inside one human
head, the different evaluations are in fact coordinated by
at least three processes in society. The first of these is
the market, which coordinates some four billion different
sets of human preferences into constantly changing patterns
of relative prices. For things that are bought and sold,
market prices are a pretty good first approximation to relative values, although they are not the same thing necessarily as social values. They are not much of a guide to
things that are not bought and sold, and there are many of
these in the evaluation of the total system. A second method of coordination is politics, the process by which powerful roles are established and individuals are placed in
them. The decisions of the powerful are limited by vanity,
by fear of losing reputation, or more negatively, by the
fear of being murdered or thrown out of office. They may be
inspired positively by the desire to do a good job. The mix
of public goods provided by the political apparatus does
change, partly in response to fairly random forces like
those which put Hitler or Amin in positions of power, but
partly also through the impact of prevailing sentiment and
political preferences. In democratic societies there is a

strong tendency for the political preferences of the middle
to dominate, for only by appealing to these can anybody get
elected. A candidate in the middle can move both ways to
acquire votes; a candidate on either the right or the left
can only move one way, as both Goldwater and McGovern discovered.

A third process of coordination is ethics, that is, the
criticism of individual preferences by people around the
individual. This is expressed in the ethos of the peer
group, conveyed in raised eyebrows, a sharp tone of voice,
abusive language, or in praise, approval, and so on. The
larger ethos of the society impinges itself on the groups
within it and also on individuals through the mass media,
books, sermons, and other larger communications. The effect
of these moral pressures is very large. Individuals whose
preferences do not conform to them either tend to be made to
conform or they break out of the group, or in extreme cases
the group segregates them; for instance, in prison or con-
centration camps. The group may even kill the dissidents
off with capital punishment or genocide. In all societies
the pressures for conformity are very large and this is
often not recognized simply because we take so much for
granted.

One of the most interesting problems in assessment is
the identification of structures and processes in society
which produce "perverse dynamics." This is what I have
called the "paradox of decision"--why is it when all decisions are for the best that situations often go from bad to
worse, even in the estimation of the decision-makers? Such
things as the tragedy of the commons, the prisoner's dilemma,
market externalities, pathologies of power (power corrupts
and so does impotence), pathologies of organization, Peter
principles and Parkinson's laws, the corruption of information by hierarchy and by deception, the fact that the per-
suasive is not always the true, and the convincing is not
always right. Then there is the dismal theorem in economics
that if only misery can check the growth of the population,
the population will grow until it is miserable. There is
also a dismal theorem of political science, that the skills
that lead to a rise to power always unfit people to exercise
it. The list is so extensive that it is amazing that any
human process ever goes from bad to better, as it surpris-
ingly often does. One of the great objects of assessment in
normative science is to identify these perverse processes
and to propose remedies for them.

The above comments were inspired, I must confess, more
by the subject than by the papers themselves, all of which,

however, I did find very interesting. My almost subconscious muse has summarized them in the course of the meeting, with, I confess, certain implicit comments in what I hope is something a little better than doggerel. These verses I append:

Joseph F. Coates

Issues are conflicts that none can resolve,
Problems are puzzles that have a solution;
Scientists try to find *issues* to *solve*,
Statesmen fight problems, and so get pollution.

Government has an orchestra of tools,
But everyone plays on the one that he pleases;
No one conducts, for that's not in the rules,
So nothing comes out but cacophonous wheezes.

Bureaucrats suffer for doing things wrong,
No one gets payoffs for doing things right,
So public efficiency goes for a song
And science illuminates only its Light.

Appealing to values is usually fudge,
Participation is mostly cosmetic;
Scientists cannot of usefulness judge,
And truth, we all fear, is a social emetic.

Kenneth R. Hammond

There must be an optimal manner of thought
In making our judgments on policy issues,
But how can this optimal manner be bought
When all that is "straight" is the flimsiest
   of tissues?

We step down the stairs of the modes of cognition
From knowledge of small things to ignorance of great;
The latter, alas, tends to lead to perdition
But alway is normal in matters of State.

So what is the answer to this giant riddle,
When knowledge is useless, and ignorance power?
The answer perhaps will be found in the middle
Where Judgment Analysis has its great hour.

Both farms and the White House are oceans of chaos,
Good management's hopeless, so here's to good luck--
Unless Hammond's organ can somehow convey us
To harmony, learning, and values unstuck.

Paul Slovic

All new technology lands us in risk
And this needs assessment by skillful assessors,
So cognitive scientists quietly frisk
The minds of the public with paper confessors. *

People are overimpressed by the visible
So that their estimates always are wrong.
People's views, even when shown to be risible,
If they are strong, will remain very strong.

Folks are prepared to buy costs for some benefits,
But costs are inflated when strange, few, and dread.
People's impressions all fit with too many fits,
And where there are devils the fools fear to tread.

In things that are sacred we ask for perfection--
A risk more than zero we cannot accept.
So unless we believe Calvinistic election,
We'll all die from fear of the slightest defect.

----
*
 questionnaires

Ward Edwards

In solving a problem or making decision
We face uncertain futures and doubtful utilities.
So all our endeavors will end in derision
Unless we can measure the true probabilities.

The Devious Director is no moral athlete,
But still he would rather do better than worse;
The Dubious Director asks "Where does the path lead
And how can I Ward off the future's dread curse?"

How do we judge the X-rays efficacious?
That's a beautiful subject for big grant submissions.
Yet to find real effects is too hard--but good
   gracious
At least we can study the doubts of physicians!

In making predictions we use probabilities,
For if we do this then we cannot be wrong,
And if multi-attributes measure utilities,
Suboptimization will soon come along.

Decision analysis soon will inform us
On how to have fatal catastrophes cheap;
But we hope that the time that it takes is
    enormous--
Then we'll have time to look, and perhaps we
    won't leap.

7

Science, Values and Human Judgment

Kenneth R. Hammond and Leonard Adelman

Scientists and policy-makers are uncertain how scientific facts are to be integrated with social values. For their part, scientists are uncertain whether their contributions should be restricted to presenting the facts, thereby leaving the policy judgment entirely to the political decision-makers, or whether they should also advise politicians which course the scientist believes to be best. And politicians, for their part, are uncertain how much scientific information they are supposed to absorb, and how much dependence they should place on scientists for guidance in reaching a judgment about policy (1). As a result, "the scientific community continues its seemingly endless debate about the role of science and scientists in the body politic" (2).

One principal reason for the "endless debate" is that scientific progress has increasingly come to be judged in the context of human values. These judgments find their ultimate expression in the forming of public policy because it is during that process that the products of science and technology are integrated, or aligned, with human values; it is during that process that scientific and technological answers to questions of what can be done are judged in the context of what ought to be done.

The key element, therefore, in the process of integrating social values and scientific facts is human judgment--a cognitive activity not directly observable and generally assumed to be recoverable only by (fallible) introspection and "self-report." These characteristics, among others, have led to the general belief that human judgment is beyond scientific analysis and therefore little has been learned about the cognitive activity that produces crucial decisions. The integration of social values and scientific information in the effort to form public policy remains largely a mystery.

The fact that an essential element in the policy formation process remains a mystery has serious consequences, one
of which is a search for safeguards. Means must be found to
avoid both poor judgments and self-serving judgments. Two
general methods have been recommended by scientists for these
purposes: (i) the adversary method, in which scientists with
differing judgments are pitted against one another in front
of a judge or jury, or both, and (ii) the search for and use
of scientists who have somehow gained a reputation for wisdom in the exercise of their judgment. Neither of these
methods provide enlightenment with regard to the judgment
process that produces the ultimate decision. Consequently,
we reject both methods because they are "ascientific"; they
leave the body politic at the mercy of a cognitive activity
which remains as much a mystery as ever.

We contend that policy judgments can be brought under
scientific study and, as a result, a process that is now
poorly understood can be examined, understood, assisted, and
thereby improved. To support this contention we describe a
scientific framework for integrating (i) scientific information (the province of scientists) and (ii) social value
judgments (the province of the electorate and their representatives) in a manner that is scientifically, socially, and
ethically defensible, and offer an example of its use.
First, however, we briefly consider two contrasting viewpoints concerning the role of science and scientists in the
body politic.

Contrasting Viewpoints of the
Role of the Scientist

There are two main viewpoints; one is that scientists
should merely present unbiased information, while the other
is that scientists should provide advice with regard to the
implications of scientific information. The first view can
be illustrated by the comments of Phillip Handler, President
of the National Academy of Sciences (NAS), in an interview
with Otten, of the Wall Street Journal. Otten (3) writes:
"Once the scientific community has presented the facts, however, it must leave final decisions to the policy-makers
and the public, Mr. Handler asserts. 'Science can contribute much to enhancing agricultural production, but American
policy with respect to food aid is not intrinsically a scientific question.' Similarly, science can study whether energy
independence is technically feasible or whether Soviet under-
ground nuclear tests can be detected, but [Handler] insists,
[scientists] must then let regular policy-makers decide
whether to try for energy independence or just what arms
control proposals to put to the Russians." Otten concluded

that "Both science and government seem well served by this reasonable man."

Handler's viewpoint as represented in the above quotation is exactly in accord with the two Executive Orders (1918, 1956) concerning the role of the National Research Council. These documents indicate that scientists are to render information to those who are entitled to receive it, but they do not imply that scientists should offer their judgment as to what public policy should follow from their studies.

In practice it may be impossible not to offer such judgments. With the ever-increasing reliance of society on science and technology it is difficult to imagine how modern scientific information could be conveyed to nonscientists without providing such judgments. In a recent editorial in Science, Boulding (4) argued that if policy judgments were not offered by scientists, they would be demanded by politicians.

> Every decision involves the selection among an agenda
> of alternative images of the future, a selection
> that is guided by some system of values. The values
> are traditionally supposed to be the cherished pre-
> serve of the political decision-maker, but the agenda,
> which involves fact or at least a projection into the
> future of what are presumably factual systems, should
> be very much in the domain of science. . . . [But] if
> the decision-maker simply does not know what the re-
> sults of alternative actions will be, it is difficult
> to evaluate unknown results. The decision-maker
> wants to know what are the choices from which he must
> choose [italics ours].

Toulmin (5, pp. 102-103) goes further than Boulding. Whereas Boulding notes that politicians may demand policy judgments from scientists, Toulmin argues that it may be part of the scientists' responsibility to offer policy judgments before such judgments are requested by political decision-makers. Thus, "In the early days, the picture was always of the politician as the man who first formulated for himself questions about the political options, about the choices he had to make: on this view, he subsequently turned to people called 'technical advisors' and asked them how to do this or that, how much each option would cost, and so on. A lot of people still see the relationship between the scientist or technologist and the politicians on this model . . . ." But, Toulmin observes, ". . . even during [World

War II] scientists were being transformed into people who
could very often see a fresh range of policy options <u>before</u>
the politicians could." Significantly, Toulmin notes that
"To some extent, the institutional relationships between
politics and science have not yet caught up with this
change."

Thus, Toulmin points out that the decision-maker not
only wants to know "the choices from which he must choose,"
as Boulding put it, but he also wants to know which choice
the scientist thinks he should choose. Senator Muskie's call
for a "one-armed scientist" (one who would not qualify his
advice with "on the other hand") exemplifies the politician's
demand for an unequivocal answer to the question of what
ought to be done as well as to that of what can be done.

This situation has not escaped the attention of students
of the role of scientists in the formation of public policy.
The presence of, the demand for, and the exercise of value
judgments has led to a sharp focus on the values, and thus
on the motives, of the scientists who participate in the
preparation of NAS reports that affect public policy.

The Focus on Scientists and Their Motives

In his book <u>The Brain Bank of America</u> (<u>6</u>, p. 54) Boffey
attributes self-serving motives to scientists who provide
information and advice to the government within the framework of NAS committees, and thus questions their objectivity
and honesty. For example:

> The Academy claims that the most distinctive feature
> of its committees is that they are independent of any
> pressures of special interests. . . . But the Acad-
> emy's record in recent years suggests that its pro-
> testations of Supreme Court impartiality should not be
> taken at face value. In actual practice, many of the
> Academy's reports have been influenced by powerful
> interests that have a stake in the questions under
> investigation.

Boffey admits, however, that "We found no cases of
direct, personal conflict of interests at the Academy--no
cases, for example, where a committee member profited
financially as a direct result of the advice he rendered"
(<u>6</u>, p. 54). The charge that "many of the Academy's reports
have been influenced by powerful interests" is directed
toward the broader social and political motives which he
claims influence scientists' judgments.

The NAS has already accepted the principle that the motives of scientists must be examined. Boffey (6, p. 87) notes with approval that the NAS demands a "bias statement" from the scientists who provide information to the government, a report that is intended to reveal one's true interests, as may be inferred from a list of "all jobs, consultantships, and directorships held for the past 10 years, all current financial interests whose market value exceeds $10,000, or 10 percent of the individual's holdings; all sources of research support for the past five years, and any other information, such as public stands on an issue which 'might appear to other reasonable individuals as compromising of your independence of judgment.' " Thus the NAS has already fallen victim to the ethic of the lawyer (and the journalist). Trust no one, is the rule, unless they can offer this negative proof: I am not now, nor have I ever been, under the control of any incentive to lie, cheat, or otherwise compromise my judgment. Whereas this approach may begin with a request for a "self-report" on sources of bias, it seldom ends there, as scientists know all too well. Investigation is undertaken by others, and by other means, precisely because the focus has been successfully turned away from methods to persons and their motives.

The results of the focus on persons and their motives can be seen in Polsby's review (7) of Boffey's book. Polsby indicates what the results might have been had he taken a similar approach in his review by raising suspicions about Boffey's impartiality and thus his motives. That is, by using "Boffey's own primary method of demonstration: a glance at somebody's background gives a 'motive' for selected characteristics of his performance," Polsby finds that "Boffey's employer for the writing of this book was Ralph Nader (identified as 'consumer champion Ralph Nader' on p. 186), who of late has gotten rather heavily into the business of sponsoring exposés of establishment-type establishments. . . . Under these circumstances of employment, could Boffey have done other than to produce an attack, no matter how flimsily founded, on the Academy?" (7, p. 666).

Polsby's review shows the customary result of such mutual destruction. Boffey's approach, he concludes, "is only good for so much mileage. . . . Arbitrarily imposing the symmetrical assumption . . . that Boffey and the Academy are both fatally incapacitated by conflict of interest has the effect of condemning both the Academy and the book out of hand" (7, p. 666). In short, because neither the critic nor those criticized can be trusted, the reader, the consumer, and the public remain buried in doubt as to where the truth lies. Thus, Polsby acknowledges that, "After reading The Brain Bank of America I do not know what to think about the Academy as an organization for evaluating the state of scientific knowledge" (7, p. 666). In all likelihood, Polsby is not the only reader of Boffey's book who no longer knows what to think about the Academy.

It is precisely because scientists have learned that it is not only fruitless, but harmful, to focus on persons and their motives that they have learned to ignore them in their work as scientists. When scientists look for the truth and the truth appears to be in doubt, neither scientific work nor the scientific ethic requires the investigation of the characteristics of the person working on the problem; instead, they require the analysis of the method by which the results are produced. Unfortunately, in the confusion of the "endless debate" there has been a tendency to forget the scientific procedure and its associated ethics. The focus on persons and their motives has led not only to the filing of bias statements but to the advocacy of the adversary method for the settlement of disputes about the truth--a method which is ascientific not only in its procedure, but in its greater commitment to victory rather than to truth.

Scientists as Adversaries

The concept of a "science court" reached Congress several years ago when Kantrowitz (8) urged that members of Congress "appoint a science advocate for (each) side of the story . . . . " He further suggested that a procedure be worked out which would be "modeled on the judicial procedure for proceeding in the presence of scientific controversy." The final judgment would be exercised by a group of scientific judges who would cross-examine each other and challenge each other's position. Kantrowitz's argument is currently being given serious consideration by members of the scientific community. Physics Today (published by the American Institute of Physics) recently indicated that a science court was worth trying, as did H. Guyford Stever, director of the National Science Foundation (9).

Members of the scientific community are not unanimous, however, in their appraisal of the value of the adversary system, as the following interchange between Platt, Dror, and Waddington in a Ciba symposium indicates (10, p. 210):

> PLATT: In the U.S. . . . we are beginning to have something called "adversary science," where scientists speak on public issues, doing their best,

like lawyers, for a particular side, and then in a
later case perhaps doing their best for the opposite
side. The hope is that in this kind of open con-
frontation, as in a court of law, one comes closer
to the truth than by having just accidents of committee structure or unanswered polemics decide the
matter.

WADDINGTON: I would strongly oppose that
way of advancing science.

PLATT: But somebody should make the total case
for a nuclear plant, and somebody should make the
total case against the plant for environmental reasons,
so that we can see all of both sides before we decide.

DROR: Why shouldn't the two sides make two balanced presentations for and against? Why total . . . ?

PLATT: Do you know a better system?

DROR: Yes, reliance on professional judges in
courts; and careful policy analysis on television for
the public.

PLATT: Who judges the judges?

DROR: Who judges the juries?

WADDINGTON: That is a piece of politics, not
a piece of learning. Learning is not advanced by
legal procedures.

The above interchange not only indicates a divergence
in viewpoint with regard to a science court and illustrates
the morass (Who judges the judges? Who judges the juries?)
into which scientists can be drawn because of the focus on
persons, but it also points to the unproductiveness of the
effort. Even if the concept of a science court were to be
accepted by scientists, and even if scientists could be per-
suaded to make the "total case for (say) a nuclear plant"
(10, p. 201), the adversary procedure would indicate only
who had been judged to be the winner in the arena of com-
peting scientific facts and scientific judgments. Integration of scientific judgments with social values would remain buried in the minds of the judges and the juries (and
their judges); the "endless debate" would not be terminated.

It remains to be seen whether a science court, with its
judges and juries and its ascientific adversary proceedings
in which one scientist is pitted against another will be
accepted by scientists. In any event, scientists not
advocating the adversary method recommend a different
ascientific method, the person-oriented approach.

Scientists' Advocacy of the
Person-Oriented Approach

When scientists have addressed themselves to the function of human judgment in policy formation they have treated
the unexamined intuitive abilities of persons as though they
were somehow superior to the scientific method. For example,
in its report on technology assessment to the House Committee
on Science and Astronautics, the Committee on Public Engineering Policy (COPEP) of the National Academy of Engineering
observed (11, p. 17) that "applying only cause-effect [i.e.,
scientific] methods to technology-initiated studies produces a mass of data but few broad conclusions." Apparently
assuming that it had no other recourse, the committee called
for ". . . contributions of talented individuals or groups
who can intuitively perform analysis and evaluations . . . ,"
an approach which "demands an integrated combination of information and value judgments that cannot always be formulated explicitly."

Not only does the COPEP report illustrate the advocacy
of a person-oriented approach to the combination of "information and value judgments" that appeals to the mysterious as
a substitute for the scientific method, it provides a clear
case of the failure to recognize that it is precisely such
person-oriented "combinations of information and value judgments that cannot always be formulated explicitly" that are
defenseless against charges of self-serving bias.

Skolnikoff and Brooks (12) were critical of the NAS
study of science and public policy-making because it suggested that persons who provide science advice should have
personal qualities of "intelligence, wisdom, judgment, humanity and perspective" on the ground that "These qualities
are so obviously desirable for anybody in a high position
that they are hardly helpful criteria." Yet they are as
willing as COPEP or the NAS committee to let the process of
combining facts and values remain subject to the unexamined
vagaries of human judgment. For example (12, p. 38):

Judgment on both technical and nontechnical issues and
on their interaction is thus required [on policy

issues]; a logically reasoned single answer is not possible. Judgment is necessarily affected by biases, policy preferences, ignorance, differing estimates of the nontechnical factors, and other vagaries. There is nothing wrong with this; it is unavoidable.

But there is something wrong with this, and this situation is avoidable. What is wrong is that both solutions indicated above focus on persons rather than on method, and both confuse scientific and valuative judgments. That is bad practice; it is bad for scientists, bad for leaders in government, and bad for the public that both are trying to serve. It is bad because it condones and encourages confusion of thought and function, substitutes an appeal to the unknown in place of the knowable, and màkes scientists easy targets for charges of self-serving bias. The argument advanced by Skolnikoff and Brooks merely puts a brave face on a bad situation, for they imply that because scientific and valuative judgments cannot be separated there is nothing wrong with confusing them. That argument suggests that if such judgments could be separated, it would be wrong to confuse them. We argue that, from the point of view of science, it is not impossible in principle or in practice to achieve such a separation (13).

A scientific approach toward the role of judgment would be quite different from the person-oriented approach that is embedded in the adversary system. A scientific approach would emphasize that judgment is a human cognitive activity and is therefore subject to scientific analysis, as are all natural phenomena. The premises of a scientific approach to the relation of science to public policy are: (i) human judgment is a critical part of the policy-making process; (ii) it is a part of the process that remains poorly understood; and (iii) it might well be improved through scientific study. Rather than searching for persons who possess mysterious talents, or indicating that the present situation is unavoidable, the scientific approach to this problem would be similar to the scientific approach to all problems: carry out theoretical and empirical analyses of the process in a manner that is subject to criticism and that provides cumulative knowledge.

The remainder of this article (i) provides an example that illustrates the social costs of employing the adversary system and the person-oriented approach and (ii) outlines a scientific framework for integrating scientific information and social values in the formation of public policy (14).

An Example of Contrasting Approaches

In 1974, the Denver Police Department (DPD), as well as other police departments throughout the country, decided to change its handgun ammunition. The principal reason offered by the police was that the conventional round-nosed bullet provided insufficient "stopping effectiveness" (that is, the ability to incapacitate and thus to prevent the person shot from firing back at a police officer or others). The DPD chief recommended (as did other police chiefs) the conventional bullet be replaced by a hollow-point bullet. Such bullets, it was contended, flattened on impact, thus decreasing penetration, increasing stopping effectiveness, and decreasing ricochet potential.

The suggested change was challenged by the American Civil Liberties Union, minority groups, and others. Opponents of the change claimed that the new bullets were nothing more than outlawed "dum-dum" bullets, that they created far more injury than the round-nosed bullet, and should, therefore, be barred from use. As is customary, judgments on this matter were formed privately and then defended publicly with enthusiasm and tenacity, and the usual public hearings were held. Both sides turned to ballistics experts for scientific information and support.

Adversary, Person-Oriented Approach

From the beginning both sides focused on the question of which bullet was best for the community. As a result of focusing on bullets and their technical ballistics characteristics, legislators and city councilmen never described the social policy that should control the use of force and injury in enforcing the law; they never specified the relative importance of the societal characteristics of bullets (injury, stopping effectiveness, or ricochet). Instead, the ballistics experts assumed that function. When the legislators requested their judgment as to which bullet was "best," the ballistics experts implicitly indicated the social policy that should be employed. That is, in recommending the use of a specific bullet, they not only implicitly recommended specific degrees of injury, stopping effectiveness, and ricochet, but also recommended a social policy regarding the relative importance of these factors. In short, the legislators' function was usurped by the ballistics experts, who thus became incompetent and unauthorized legislators--incompetent because of their lack of information about the social and political context in which a choice would be made; unauthorized because they assumed a function for which they had not been elected.

In parallel fashion, the ballistics experts turned their scientific-technical function over to those who should have formed social policy--the legislators. When the experts presented scientific information to policy-makers about various bullets, they found themselves disputing ballistics data with legislators who preferred a different type of bullet. Thus, the legislators, none of whom were ballistics experts, in their turn served as incompetent ballistics experts in the hearings.

When legislators and scientists accept the adversary system with its concomitant person-oriented approach as the primary means for integrating science and social values, they may expect to find a reversal of roles, and when scientists accept the person-oriented approach they may expect to be confronted by challenges to their objectivity (15). The outcome is well represented by the comment of one legislator who said to an opponent (16): "You have your expert and we have ours. . . ."

A Scientific Approach

We now consider, by way of an example, a scientific method for integrating scientific information and social values that is scientifically, socially, and ethically defensible. This method was employed in solving the dispute about handgun ammunition for the police as described above. A broad outline of the method is presented (17).

The general framework of the method as it was applied to the above problem is shown in Fig. 1. Basic to any policy involving scientific information are objectively measurable variables (Fig. 1, left). Scientific judgments regarding the potential effects of technological alternatives are also required (Fig. 1, middle). Finally, social value judgments by policy-makers or community representatives are necessary (Fig. 1, right). The overall acceptability of an alternative is determined by how closely its potential effects satisfy the social values of the community.

Application of this framework to the bullet dispute involved three phases: (i) externalization of social value judgments; (ii) externalization of scientific judgments; and (iii) integration of social values and scientific judgments. Each phase is discussed in turn.

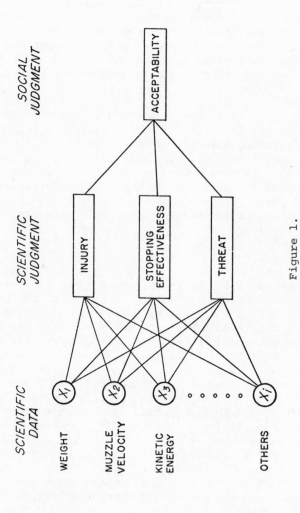

Figure 1.

Phase 1: Externalizing social value judgments.
The participants in phase 1 included the mayor and city
council, other elected officials, representatives of the
DPD (including the chief), and official representatives of
community organizations, including minority groups and members of the general public. Each person was asked to make
judgments concerning the relative desirability of hypothetical bullets, described in terms of their (i) stopping
effectiveness, (ii) severity of injury, and (iii) threat to
bystanders. These value judgments were made at the console
of an interactive computer terminal. After their judgments
were made, the participants were immediately shown the relative importance they gave to each of these three functional
characteristics of bullets. That is, a statistical analysis
was carried out on the data and the results were then dis-
played at the terminal for the participant to observe (18).
In addition, each participant was shown the form of the relation (linear, curvilinear) between his or her judgment and
each of the three characterisitics mentioned above. In this
way, each participant saw the relative importance he or she
attached to stopping effectiveness, injury, and threat to
bystanders, as well as the optimal point for each (a typical
display is shown in Fig. 2).

After viewing the display, the participants were asked
if the results reflected their considered judgment. The
data, corrected when necessary, were then stored, and a
cluster analysis was carried out in order to discover
whether different groups held different judgment policies.
Widely differing policies with regard to the relative importance of each characteristic were found, although the
functional relations between bullet characteristics and
judgments were all found to be approximately linear in form.

The above procedure provides objective, visible data
not otherwise available. The same procedure was used to
externalize the required scientific judgments.

Phase 2: Externalizing scientific judgments. A panel
was assembled that included one firearms expert, one ballistics expert, and three medical experts in wound ballistics. The judgments of these experts provided scientific
information regarding the stopping effectiveness, severity
of injury, and threat to bystanders of 80 bullets. The
data for these bullets were obtained from the National Bu-
reau of Standards. Each dimension (stopping effectiveness,
injury, and threat to bystanders) was judged separately for
each of the 80 bullets; agreement among the experts was
found to be quite high (19). Only the results for stopping

```
RELATIVE WEIGHT PROFILE

A : JUDGMENT
0.0------------------0.5------------------1.0      WEIGHT    FN FORM

INJURY
AAAAAAAAAAAAAAAAAA                                  .41      NEGLIN


STOP-EFFEC
AAAAAAAAAAAAAAA                                     .34      NONLIN


THREAT-BYS
AAAAAAAAAA                                          .24      NONLIN


0.0------------------0.5------------------1.0
POLICY              CONSISTENCY
JUDGMENT               .95
```

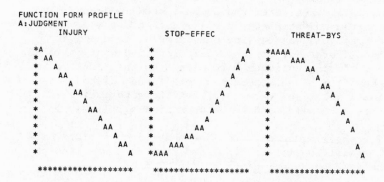

Figure 2.

effectiveness and injury are summarized here, as these were the central factors in the controversy.

Three factors were found to be important in judgments of stopping effectiveness: (i) The maximum diameter of the temporary wound cavity; (ii) the amount of kinetic energy lost by the bullet in the target; and (iii) the muzzle velocity of the bullet. The close, but not perfect, relation between stopping effectiveness and injury (shown in Fig. 3) is reflected in the fact that independent judgments of potential injury were positively related to the amount of kinetic energy lost, maximum diameter of the temporary cavity, and degree of penetration.

The data in Fig. 3 are important because they suggest that, contrary to previous, unexamined assumption, there is not a perfect relation between stopping effectiveness and injury; increasing one does not necessarily increase the other. These data illustrate the value of scientific information by indicating the possibility of finding a bullet that increases stopping effectiveness without increasing injury ([20]).

Phase 3:   Integrating social values and scientific information. Social value judgments and scientific judgments were combined by means of the equation in Fig. 4, where the separation and combination of the judgments of policy-makers and scientists-technologists may be seen. We used the following algebraic form of this equation

$$Y_s = W_1 X_1 + W_2 X_2 + W_3 X_3$$

where Y_s is the overall acceptability of a bullet; $W_j, j = 1, 3$, indicates the weight, or relative importance policy-makers placed on stopping effectiveness, injury and threat to bystanders; and $X_j, j = 1, 3$ are the experts' judgments regarding stopping effectiveness, injury, and threat to bystanders.

Because phase 1 resulted in a variety of different weights on stopping effectiveness, injury, and threat to bystanders, the city council took all three factors into consideration by placing equal weight on each. As a result, when considering stopping effectiveness and severity of injury only, the appropriate bullet is one which lies farthest from the line of average relation in Fig. 3, this distance from the line being measured perpendicularly from the point to the line. Bullet 9 in Fig. 3 satisfies this criterion. It has greater stopping effectiveness and is less apt to cause injury (and less apt to threaten bystanders) than the

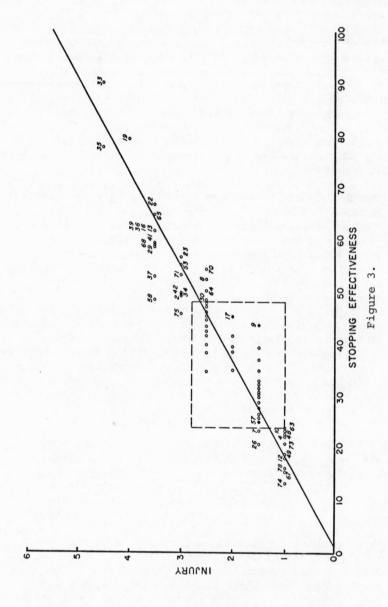

Figure 3.

standard bullet then in use by the DPD (bullet 57). In addition, bullet 9 (a hollow-point bullet) is less apt to cause injury than is bullet 17, the hollow-point bullet recommended by the DPD. Bullet 9 was accepted by the city council and all other parties concerned, and is now being used by the DPD (21).

Finally, three points should be mentioned with regard to the application of judgment analysis to the above problem.

1) Intense political and social conflict existed prior to our participation in the project. During the controversy a Denver police officer was killed by a hollow-point bullet; as a result, hundreds of policemen staged a march that ended in demands on both the police chief and the governor that the police be permitted to use hollow-point bullets. Members of the city council and others seemed convinced that the usual adversary methods had failed, and that they faced a dangerous impasse. The fact that the above procedures were used in these circumstances indicates that elected officials and special interest groups can accept a scientific approach to critical social problems, even when they have become immersed in sharp political dispute. Moreover, interviews with members of the city council and others not only indicated a high degree of satisfaction with the procedure but appreciation of its impersonal approach as well.

2) The procedures were applied to complex technical judgments. As far as we could determine, at the time of the research no standard quantifiable definition of severity of injury (with regard to handgun ammunition) had ever been developed. Moreover, in developing such a definition, and in making their judgments, the ballistics experts considered 11 distinct characteristics of handgun ammunition.

3) The procedure is general in nature. Despite the apparent simplicity of the framework presented in Fig. 4, judgment analysis can be applied to a variety of complex problems involving value judgments and scientific judgments by differentiating the elements in Fig. 4 in a hierarchical fashion (22).

Scientific defensibility. The above method is scientifically defensible, not because it is flawless (it isn't), but because it is readily subject to scientific criticism. It is vulnerable to such criticism (i) because its aim is to meet appropriate standards regarding replication, quantification, and logic for the problem under study (an aim all

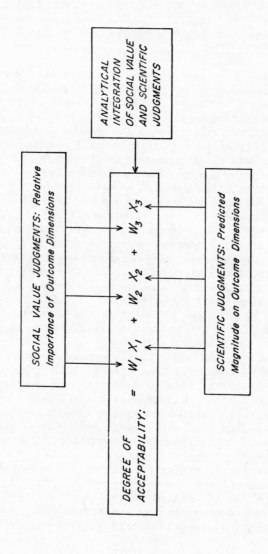

Figure 4.

scientific efforts share) and (ii) because the procedure
for achieving that aim is public (as all scientific effort
must be). The locus and degree of imperfection in method
and procedure are thus available for public inspection and
subsequent improvement. In short, the process provides the
opportunity for cumulative knowledge, as scientific efforts
should.

Social responsibility. The above method is socially
responsible because it provides a public framework for (i)
separating technical, scientific judgment from social value
judgments and (ii) integrating them analytically, not judg-
mentally. The separation phase permits elected representatives to function exclusively as policy-makers, and scientists to function exclusively as scientists. Neither role
is confused or exchanged because policy-makers are not forced
to become amateur scientists, nor are scientists required to
make judgments on public policy. The integrative phase provides an overt, rather than covert, process for combining
facts and values. Because the social values in the community are identified before the decision is implemented, the
decision process is not seen to be a mere defense of a pre-
determined choice; rather it can be evaluated in terms of its
rational basis before the final choice is made.

Ethical standards. Ethical and scientific standards
converge in the process of combining facts and values because both scientific ethics and public ethics require controls against bias. Scientific control against bias is
illustrated by the use of the double-blind control in experiments; in the above procedure public control against bias
is carried out by a similar blindness. That is, the method
described above has the advantage of situating all parties
(policy-makers, scientists, and the public) behind what
Rawls (23, p. 136) calls "a veil of ignorance." It fits
Rawls' requirement that the participants should not "know
how the various alternatives [would] affect their own particular case and they are obliged to evaluate principles
solely on the basis of general considerations." In the
approach described above, the technical experts were not
aware of the relative importance the policy-makers placed on
the three societal characteristics of bullets, nor were the
policy-makers aware of the technical judgments made by the
scientists-technologists in regard to specific bullets. In
short, by implementing Rawls' veil of ignorance, both scientific and ethical standards were met.

Conclusion

Current efforts to integrate scientific information and social values in the forming of public policy are confused and defeated by the widespread use of ascientific methods-- the adversary system and the person-oriented approach. The adversary system suffers from an ascientific commitment to victory rather than truth; the person-oriented approach suffers from an ascientific focus on persons and their motives rather than on the adequacy of methods. The reason for the widespread use of both lies in the failure to recognize that human judgment can be brought under scientific, rather than ad hominem, analysis. The argument advanced here is that a scientifically, socially, and ethically defensible means for integrating science and human values can be achieved.

References and Notes

1. See, for example, Public Law 92-484 which established the Office of Technology Assessment.
2. J.W. Curlin, Science 190, 839 (1975).
3. A.L. Otten, Wall Street Journal, 3 April 1975, p. 12.
4. K.E. Boulding, Science 190, 423 (1975).
5. S.E. Toulmin, in Civilization and Science: In Conflict or Collaboration?, Ciba Foundation Symposium 1 (Elsevier, Amsterdam, 1972).
6. P. Boffey, The Brain Bank of America (McGraw-Hill, New York, 1975).
7. N.W. Polsby, Science 190, 665 (1975).
8. Hearings before the House Committee on Rules and Administration (1971).
9. See the article by J.N. Wilford, New York Times, 19 February 1976, p. 3.
10. The Future as an Academic Discipline, Ciba Foundation Symposium 36, (Elsevier, Amsterdam, 1975).
11. Committee on Public Engineering Policy, National Academy of Engineering, A Study of Technology Assessment (Government Printing Office, Washington, D.C., 1969).
12. E.B. Skolnikoff and H. Brooks, Science 187, 35 (1975).
13. There are clear indications that scientists are beginning to acknowledge the need for explicit methods for decision-making in areas where science and the public interest intersect. Two recent NAS committee reports [Environmental Impact of Stratospheric Flight (1975); Decision Making for Regulating Chemicals in the Environment (1975)] as well as others mentioned in the latter describe the application of normative decision theory to such problems. Although these efforts

represent a clear step forward through their insistence on the use of an explicit framework for decisions, they do not indicate how such decisions might be assisted or improved through the study of human judgment.

14. For a general review of current research on judgment and decision-making see [P. Slovic, B. Fischhoff, S. Lichtenstein, in The Annual Revivew of Psychology (Annual Reviews, Palo Alto, Calif., in press), vol 28]. See also M. Kaplan and S. Schwartz, Eds., Human Judgment and Decision Processes (Academic Press, New York, 1975); W. Edwards, M. Guttentag, K. Snapper, in Handbook of Evaluation Research, E.L. Struening and M. Guttentag, Eds. (Sage, Beverly Hills, Calif., 1975), vol 1; R.A. Howard, in Proceedings of the Fourth International Conference on Operational Research (Wiley-Interscience, New York, 1966); H. Raiffa, Decision Analysis: Introductory Lectures on Choices Under Uncertainty (Addison-Wesley, Reading, Mass., 1968).

15. Can the adversary system produce this confusion of roles at the national level, and does it have similar negative effects? Apparently it can, and does. For example, in Polsby's review of Boffey's book, Polsby (7, p. 666) states: "Boffey notes, in criticizing a National Academy of Engineering committee on pollution abatement, that it was no more qualified than any other group of citizens to judge what should be 'wise' public policy." (In this instance, Boffey argues that scientists overstepped their bounds and should have confined their role to presenting the facts.) "Sound doctrine," observes Polsby, "and yet Boffey criticizes another of the Academy's committees for taking on an assignment pertinent to a naval communications project that did not include evaluating its 'desirability,' and for not venturing to raise 'questions as to the basic worth' of the space shuttle program." (In this instance, Boffey argues that scientists failed to help form social policy and thus failed in their responsibility to the public.) Thus, concludes Polsby, "the Academy is damned if it does pronounce on the overall wisdom of public policies, and damned if it doesn't."

16. Public Broadcasting Service, "Black Horizons," 16 February 1975.

17. K.R. Hammond, T.R. Stewart, L. Adelman, N. Wascoe, Report to the Denver City Council and Mayor Regarding the Choice of Handgun Ammunition for the Denver Police Department (Report No. 179, University of Colorado, Institute of Behavioral Science, Program of Research on Human Judgment and Social Interaction, Boulder, 1975).

18. To determine the relative importance a person places on
    each characteristic, linear multiple regression analysis
    was performed to obtain the beta weights on each of the
    three judgment dimensions, or factors. The absolute
    value of the beta weight for a factor was then divided
    by the sum of the absolute values of the beta weights
    over all factors to determine the relative weight, or
    importance placed on each factor. The relative weights
    were displayed on the computer console. For technical
    details on the procedure see [K.R. Hammond, T.R. Stewart,
    B. Brehmer, D.O. Steinmann, in Human Judgment and De-
    cision Processes, M. Kaplan and S. Schwartz, Eds. (Ac-
    acemic Press, New York, 1975)].

19. The judgment dimensions were defined as follows.
    (i) Stopping effectiveness: the probability that a 20-
    to 40-year old man of average height (5' 10") and weight
    (175 lbs) shot in the torso would be incapacitated and
    rendered incapable of returning fire. Judgments ranged
    from 0 to 100, indicating, on the average, how many men
    out of 100 would be stopped by a given bullet. (ii) Se-
    verity of injury: the probability that a man, as des-
    cribed above, shot in the torso would die within 2 weeks
    of being shot. (iii) Threat to bystanders: penetration
    was defined as the probability that a bullet would pose
    a hazard to others after passing through a person shot
    in the torso at a distance of 21 feet. Ricochet was
    defined as the probability that a bullet would pose a
    hazard after missing the intended target at a distance
    of 21 feet.

20. The separation of stopping effectiveness from injury that
    is indicated in the graph for bullet 9 was not due to
    inconsistencies and inaccuracies in the experts' ratings.
    The three medical experts agreed that the shape of the
    temporary cavity is an indicator of differences in se-
    verity of injury for bullets with the same stopping
    effectiveness. More severe wounds are produced by bul-
    lets that have a long, wide temporary cavity; less se-
    vere wounds localize the maximum diameter of their
    temporary cavity and do not penetrate deeply. According
    to all three experts, a temporary cavity that reaches a
    maximum diameter of 10 to 15 cm at 5 to 7 cm from the
    surface, and does not penetrate more than 15 cm, would
    provide the best compromise between stopping effective-
    ness and survivability.

21. The time, manpower, and cost of the handgun study were as follows. (i) The project was completed in 6 weeks and (ii) research personnel included four people of whom one worked full time. Total cost, including salaries of the project staff, did not exceed $6000; an additional $3500 was required to pay the travel and consulting costs of the ballistics experts.

22. For examples of the application of a hierarchical framework, see K.R. Hammond, J. Rohrbaugh, J. Mumpower, L. Adelman, in Human Judgment and Decision Processes: Applications in Problem Settings, M.F. Kaplan and S. Schwartz, Eds. (Academic Press, New York, 1976).

23. J. Rawls, A Theory of Justice (Harvard Univ. Press, Cambridge, Mass., 1971).

24. Supported by National Institute of Mental Health grant MH-16437. We thank S. Cook, D. Deane, and B. Fischhoff, among many others, for their help.

8

Decision Errors and Fallible Judgment: Implications for Social Policy

Hillel J. Einhorn

Abstract

Although psychologists have spent a good deal of time in
documenting the fallibility of judgment, less attention has
been devoted to the effects that fallible judgments have on
decision making. In order to investigate this, the number
and types of decision errors are considered within the following task: a population of applicants applies for some
action (welfare, food stamps, medical care, etc.). Because
the action cannot be given to all who apply, a judgment (x)
must be made regarding the degree of "deservedness" of the
applicants. On this basis, people are either accepted or rejected. At some later point in time, a criterion (y) is used
to assess the accuracy of judgment and to define errors. In
order to deal analytically with the number and types of
errors, a simple probability model is developed. The model
allows one to show the relationship between the number of
acceptance errors (e.g., welfare cheaters, unnecessary surgeries, etc.) and rejection errors (people cheated out of
welfare, etc.). The trade-off relationship between these
errors is defined as is the percent of errors made relative
to the total number of decisions. These variables are then
shown as a function of the fallibility of judgment, the unconditional probability of acceptance, and the base rate,
i.e., the unconditional probability of "true need." The results are discussed with respect to the following issues:
(a) How valid must judgment be before errors can be reduced
significantly? (b) How does the fallibility of judgment and
the probability of acceptance affect the trade-off between
errors? (c) What defines "good" as opposed to "poor" decision performance? (d) Is it "worth it" to try to increase
judgmental accuracy? (e) How does the probability of acceptance reflect the differential costs of acceptance and rejection errors? (f) Is welfare cheating, unnecessary surgery,
etc., necessary? (g) If one is truly deserving (or

undeserving) how likely is it to be accepted? (h) How do outcomes based on decisions at one time affect the fate of programs over longer time periods?

Introduction

In a large American city, the local conservative newspaper does a series of stories on welfare cheaters. The paper documents many cases of people receiving welfare who are not entitled to it. Readers of the newspaper are angered by the apparent waste of tax dollars and the inefficiency of the local welfare agencies. Because of intense political pressure, the mayor orders a commission to be set up to investigate the scandal. As the commission is being formed, the local liberal newspaper launches a series of stories on the poverty-stricken and destitute who, while entitled to welfare, are not getting it. The readers of this newspaper are angered by the inefficiency of the welfare agencies and they demand that a commission be set up to find out why heartless welfare officials are not doing their jobs.

The above story is fictional although the basic issues that are raised occur with such regularity that readers can no doubt find many real life parallels. It is therefore surprising that despite the frequency of such public debates, the relationship between decision errors and the judgments that determine decisions has not been adequately explored (cf. Hammond & Adelman, 1976). While psychologists have spent a good deal of time and effort in studying judgment and documenting its fallibility (e.g., Edwards, 1968; Slovic, 1972; Tversky & Kahneman, 1974), the effects that result from using judgment for decision making purposes have been slighted (cf. Elstein, 1976). The purpose of this paper is to examine this issue by trying to answer the following question: Since judgment is often used as the basis for making decisions, how does the fallibility of judgment affect the number and types of decision errors that can be made? In answering this question, the various factors that are typically implicit in the decision process are made explicit. Therefore, many political issues become apparent although "trapped administrators" (Campbell, 1969) may be intuitively aware of much that follows.

Before beginning the analysis, it is necessary to raise an important question, viz., why not make full use of decision theory rather than concentrating on decision errors? While decision theory has proved to be useful for studying various conceptual issues, its Achilles' heel (Cronbach & Gleser, 1965) has been, and continues to be, the measurement of utility. This problem is exacerbated if one is interested

in discussing decisions such as who should receive welfare,
food stamps, special education, etc. As soon as the quality
of human life is involved, assigning utility (or dollar values) to outcomes is bound to cause controversy. By focusing
on decision errors one avoids the necessity of <u>directly</u> estimating all utilities. However, one must substitute a different and difficult set of questions that must be answered.
For example, consider the welfare decision. Rather than ask
what the utilities are for giving welfare to those that need
it, not giving it to those who do not need it, etc., the focus on decision errors asks: How many welfare cheaters is
one willing to have for every person cheated out of welfare?
While this question may not be easy to answer, it would seem
to be easier than estimating utilities for action-outcome
combinations. Part of the reason for believing this concerns
the fact that people have less difficulty in comparing things
of the same kind (Slovic & McPhillamy, 1974)--in this case,
errors. Therefore, an administrator might say that he'd be
willing to endure the cost of two welfare cheaters for not
missing someone who needs welfare. In addition to the fact
that trade-offs between errors can be understood, a second
reason for dealing with decision errors is that they are
typically used as the criterion for evaluating any program.
Decision errors are important because politicians have made
them important. Therefore, woe to the administrator who ig-
nores them.

Structure of the Task

The kinds of situations that are of concern here can be
classified broadly as selection decisions. By this is meant
the following: a population applies for some action. Because the action cannot be given to all who apply, only those
most deserving can receive it. Therefore, on the basis of
information (however collected), a judgment (x) is made concerning the degree to which various people are deserving.
Those judged to be undeserving do not receive the action
(they are rejected). It is assumed that there is a cutoff
point on x, x_c, that discriminates the "accepts" from the
"rejects." Therefore, the task is formally defined as:

$$\text{If } x \geq x_c \quad \text{accept} \quad (A)$$
$$\text{If } x < x_c \quad \text{reject} \quad (R)$$

(1)

Although (1) clearly applies to job hiring, student selection, job promotion, and the like, it also applies to applicants for welfare, food stamps, loan programs, medical care,
government grants, and journal publication (to name a few).
Clearly, selection decisions are quite general. Furthermore,

although a judgment may depend on many pieces and types of information, this information is typically combined into an overall global evaluation that determines the decision.

In order to define decision errors as well as the degree of fallibility of judgment, it is necessary that some standard or criterion be available. Clearly, a criterion (y) is not available before the judgment is made (since that would render the judgment unnecessary). However, after a decision is made, more information is typically available so that y may be inferred. For example, a doctor may accept someone for surgery only to find that during the surgery, the organ thought to be diseased was actually healthy. This would clearly be a case of an unnecessary surgery. In one sense the conceptual definition of the criterion is synonymous with the "true" score that x is trying to measure. However, the fallibility of judgment is conceptualized as the validity of judgment rather than its reliability (although the latter sets bounds on the former). While the practical difficulties of finding and developing adequate criteria are enormous, the present discussion centers on the theoretical issues that arise after these difficulties have been overcome (or at least alleviated). In order to be consistent with the formulation of judgment, it is assumed that the criterion has a cutoff point (y_c) such that $y \geq y_c$ and $y < y_c$ serve as the basis for evaluating the accuracy of judgment. Furthermore, it is assumed that the accept or reject decision does not, <u>in itself</u>, affect the score on y; i.e., the accept-reject decision does not have an experimental treatment effect. Therefore, we do not consider situations where people are accepted for some remedial action designed to increase (or decrease) their y scores. Such situations confound the effects of judgmental accuracy and experimental treatments and inflate the accuracy of judgment.[1]

A Selection-Probability Model

In order to deal with the number and types of decision errors, consider the four possible action-outcome combinations that can result from an accept/reject decision. Figure 1 shows these four combinations. First, consider if someone is accepted (i.e., $x \geq x_c$). There are two possible outcomes given the decision to accept--the person is deserving ($y > y_c$) or not ($y < y_c$). The former outcome is called a "positive hit," and the latter a "false positive" (i.e., the judgment was positive, $x \geq x_c$ and the true need wasn't, $y < y_c$). If someone is rejected ($x < x_c$), there are again two possible outcomes: the person is below or above the cut-off value of true need. The former outcome is called a

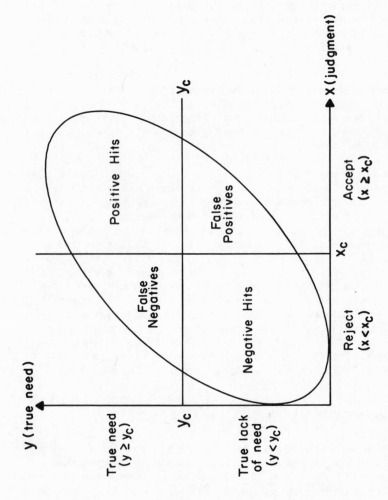

Figure 1: Action-outcome combinations that result from using judgment to make an accept/reject decision.

"negative hit" and the latter outcome a "false negative."
This model shows that one will make two kinds of errors in
any selection decision, false positives and false negatives.
For the sake of brevity, a false positive mistake will be
called an "acceptance error" and a false negative will be
called a "rejection error." Since the number of errors is of
concern, the following notation is introduced: let,

N_t = total number of applicants

N_a = number of acceptance errors, i.e., number of people
accepted who should have been rejected (welfare
cheaters, unnecessary surgeries, etc.)

N_r = number of rejection errors, i.e., number of people
rejected who should have been accepted (people
cheated out of welfare, necessary surgeries not
given, etc.).

The following probabilities are now introduced so that the
number and types of errors can be derived. Let,

$$p(x \geq x_c) = \phi = \text{selection ratio}$$

$$p(y \geq y_c) = br = \text{base rate} \quad .$$

The selection ratio indicates the unconditional probability
of acceptance while the base rate indicates the unconditional probability of "true need," or "true deservedness." In
addition to these unconditional probabilities, the probability of any action-outcome combination can also be defined;
i.e.,

$$p(y \geq y_c | x \geq x_c) = ph = \text{positive hit rate}$$

$$p(y < y_c | x \geq x_c) = fp = \text{false positive rate}$$

$$p(y < y_c | x < x_c) = nh = \text{negative hit rate}$$

$$p(y \geq y_c | x < x_c) = fn = \text{false negative rate} \quad .[2]$$

Note that,

$$ph = 1 - fp; \quad nh = 1 - fn \quad .$$

These conditional probabilities refer to the four possible
action-outcome combinations shown in Figure 1. (The use of
the term "rate" is used to distinguish the probability of an
action-outcome combination from an instance of any combination.)

Consider the errors, N_a and N_r:

$$N_a = N_t \; p(y < y_c \cap x \geq x_c) \; . \qquad (2)$$

However,

$$p(y < y_c \cap x \geq x_c) = p(y < y_c | x \geq x_c) p(x \geq x_c) \; .$$

Therefore,

$$N_a = N_t \; p(y < y_c | x \geq x_c) p(x \geq x_c) = N_t (fp)(\phi) \; . \qquad (3)$$

Similarly,

$$N_r = N_t \; p(y \geq y_c \cap x < x_c) = N_t (fn)(1 - \phi) \; . \qquad (4)$$

One would like to express N_r as a function of N_a. This has the advantage of determining the exact relationship between the numbers of both types of errors. In order to derive this, note that:

$$p(y \geq y_c) = p(y \geq y_c | x \geq x_c) p(x \geq x_c)$$
$$+ p(y \geq y_c | x < x_c) p(x < x_c) \qquad (5)$$
$$br = ph(\phi) + fn(1 - \phi) \; .$$

Now solve for fn and substitute $(1 - fp)$ for ph:

$$fn = \frac{br - \phi(1 - fp)}{(1 - \phi)} \; . \qquad (6)$$

Substituting (6) into (4) yields:

$$N_r = N_t br - N_t \phi + N_t \phi fp \; . \qquad (7)$$

However, from (3), substitute for $N_t \phi fp$ to get:

$$N_r = N_t (br - \phi) + N_a \; . \qquad (8)$$

Equation (8) is interesting for a number of reasons:

1. In any given situation, $N_r = N_a + C$, where $C =$ constant. The sign of the constant is determined solely by $(br - \phi)$. If $br > \phi$, it must be the case that $N_r > N_a$; if $br < \phi$, then $N_a > N_r$; if $br = \phi$, $N_r = N_a$. This means that in any decision, whether one makes more acceptance errors or rejection errors depends on the difference between the selection ratio and the base rate, i.e., the difference between the proportion that get the treatment (ϕ) and the proportion that "deserve" it (br).

2. While it will be shown later that (8) holds for any given degree of fallibility of judgment, the difficulty of seeing the tradeoff between N_a and N_r exists because increases (or decreases) in N_a also affect the C term. Therefore, another way to look at the tradeoff between the errors is given by their ratio, i.e.,

$$N_a/N_r = \frac{fp(\phi)}{fn(1 - \phi)} \quad \text{(divide (3) by (4))} \quad . \quad (9)$$

The ratio shows that <u>both</u> the fallibility of judgment and the selection ratio determine the tradeoff between the two types of errors. For example, consider that in the welfare decision, $N_a/N_r = .5$ (e.g., this could occur if $fp = .1$, $fn = .2$, $\phi = .5$). This would mean that for every welfare cheat there are two people being cheated out of welfare. Knowledge of (9) would seem to be of great importance to administrators, politicians, and the public. It seems likely that large differences in opinion will exist concerning what this ratio <u>should be</u>. (As a matter of fact, different values of this ratio may define the difference between conservatives and liberals.) However, unless one knows what this ratio is (or will be), manipulation of ϕ, for example, to change the situation may lead to less rather than more desirable results. This will be shown in greater detail later in the paper.

It is important to note that (8) and (9) express somewhat different aspects of the same problem. Equation (8) deals with the absolute number of both kinds of errors while (9) expresses the implicit tradeoff between them. Both of these factors are important. Moreover, both equations call attention to the importance of the ϕ variable. For example, if ϕ were set equal to the base rate, from (8), $N_a = N_r$ and therefore, $N_a/N_r = 1.0$. An administrator who followed such a strategy should be aware that it implies that the two types of errors are being treated equally. Furthermore, this particular result holds regardless of how fallible the judgment is.

The last measure that is defined concerns the total number of errors made relative to the number of decisions. Therefore, this is simply the percent total errors, i.e.,

$$\% \text{ errors} = (N_a + N_r)/N_t \quad . \quad (10)$$

Fallibility of Judgment

In order to formally incorporate the idea of fallibility into the analysis, some measure of it is necessary. In

Table 1

Error Indices as a Function of Judgment Fallibility:

$N_t = 1,000,000$; $br = .30$; $\phi = .20$

(1) ρ_{xy}	(2) N_a	(3) ph	(4) N_r	(5) nh	(6) N_a/N_r	(7) % errors	(8) $p(A|y \geq y_c)$	(9) $p(A|y < y_c)$
.00	140,000	.30	240,000	.70	.58	38.0	.20	.20
.10	130,000	.35	230,000	.71	.56	36.0	.23	.19
.20	120,000	.40	220,000	.73	.55	34.0	.27	.17
.30	108,000	.46	208,000	.74	.52	31.6	.31	.16
.40	98,000	.51	198,000	.75	.50	29.6	.34	.14
.50	84,000	.58	184,000	.77	.46	26.8	.39	.11
.60	72,000	.64	172,000	.78	.42	24.4	.43	.10
.70	56,000	.72	156,000	.81	.36	21.2	.48	.08
.80	40,000	.80	140,000	.82	.29	18.0	.53	.06
.90	20,000	.90	120,000	.85	.17	14.0	.60	.03
1.00	0	1.00	100,000	.88	0	10.0	.67	.00

studies dealing with clinical judgment, the accuracy of judgment has typically been measured by the correlation between judgment and criterion (ρ_{xy}). This measure is used here primarily because it allows one to see the implications of previous research with respect to the number and types of decision errors, tradeoffs, etc. Furthermore, the correlation coefficient is widely used by many researchers so that it is not only familiar, but people have had experience with respect to the values it takes in practice. It is now necessary to translate the fallibility of judgment, as measured by ρ_{xy}, into probabilities that can be used in the earlier section. In order to do this, two assumptions are necessary: (1) x and y are distributed as a bivariate normal distribution. This implies that they are linearly related; (2) x and y are standardized variables.

Consider the regression of y on x, where the intersection of x_c and y_c results in areas that correspond to the various hit and error rates (see Figure 1). Given the above two assumptions, any combination of ρ_{xy}, ϕ, and br determines ph, nh, fp, and fn (see footnote 3). Therefore, the various probabilities needed to compute the error indices defined earlier can be obtained. The importance of this is that it is then possible to study the effects of the degree of fallibility of judgment as well as the effects of different base rates and selection ratios on the various error indices. In order to illustrate, consider the following example: assume that there are 1,000,000 applicants for welfare in a particular area ($N_t = 1,000,000$). Furthermore, assume that we have some estimate of "true need" as being .30, i.e., br = .30. Finally, assume that because of budgetary constraints, we can only accept .20 of those applying (ϕ = .20). Given the above information, one can calculate the various error indices as a function of ρ_{xy}. This is done for values of ρ_{xy} that vary from 0 to 1.0 in increments of .1. These results are shown in Table 1.

The first column in Table 1 shows the fallibility of judgment as measured by ρ_{xy}. Column 2 gives the number of acceptance errors as a function of ρ_{xy}. Clearly, as ρ_{xy} increases, N_a decreases (although not by a constant amount). The third column shows the probability of deserving welfare given that one gets it. This probability is simply the positive hit rate (ph). For example, if ρ_{xy} = .40, the probability of a correct decision for those getting welfare is only .51. Of course, this means that almost half the people given welfare don't deserve it (98,000/200,000). Note that the probability of making a correct accept decision does not increase greatly until $\rho_{xy} > .70$. One advantage of seeing these probabilities in tabular form is that baseline performance (when $\rho_{xy} = 0$) can be seen and used for comparison purposes. Therefore, although ph is .51 when $\rho_{xy} = .4$, one can see that the value of ph when $\rho_{xy} = 0$ is .30. The fourth column shows the number of rejection errors. It will be remembered that N_r can be expressed as a function of N_a by equation (8). For the particular set of values used in this example,

$$N_r = 100,000 + N_a \quad .$$

Note that the linear relationship holds over all values of ρ_{xy} (the linear relationship is general over all combinations of br and ϕ). Since $\phi <$ br (in this example), although there are many welfare cheats (for $\rho_{xy} \neq 1.0$), there are many more people being cheated out of welfare. It seems that the liberal and conservative newspapers are right. It is important to note that results such as these arise from the fact that human judgment is fallible (and, in this case, that $\phi \neq$ br). Attributions about the "heartlessness" of welfare administrators may be unjustified without further evidence. (Of course, examples where $\phi >$ br could lead to attributions of "bleeding heart" liberalism of the same administrators.) Finally, note that even if $\rho_{xy} = 1.0$, since $\phi <$ br, there are still 100,000 rejection errors. Therefore, as long as br $\neq \phi$, infallibility of judgment ($\rho_{xy} = 1.0$) does not mean error-free decisions.

Column (5) shows the probability of making a correct reject decision (this is simply the negative hit rate, nh). For the values of ϕ and br used here, it is interesting to note the insensitivity of this probability to reductions in the fallibility of judgment. Column (6) shows the trade-off relationship between the two types of errors. It will be recalled from (9) that this ratio is a function of both the fallibility of judgment and ϕ. The effect of ρ_{xy} can be seen quite clearly--as ρ_{xy} increases, the ratio decreases. This means that as the accuracy of judgment increases (when $\phi <$ br), one will make more reject errors per accept error (although the number of each type of error decreases). The reason for the change in N_a/N_r with ρ_{xy} is due to the fact that N_r is a linear function of N_a. Therefore, as N_a decreases, N_r decreases but the percent change is less, changing the ratio. In cases where $\phi >$ br, increasing ρ_{xy} leads to increasing N_a/N_r ratios, i.e., more accept errors per reject error. It is interesting to remember that when $\phi =$ br, $N_a/N_r = 1.0$ at all levels of the fallibility of judgment. Therefore, the fallibility of judgment affects the tradeoff between errors whenever $\phi \neq$ br.

Column (7) shows the percent total errors. Examination of this factor brings up an interesting point concerning the sensitivity of the results to ρ_{xy}. While the percent total errors seems to be a relatively flat function of ρ_{xy} note that because of the large number of decisions to be made, the decrease in the number of errors is substantial. For example, consider the increase of ρ_{xy} from .3 to .7. While the gain in explained variance increases by five times, the percent errors only decreases by 10 per cent. However, this modest percent improvement is translated into making over 100,000 fewer mistakes. When the results are viewed in this way, increasing the validity of judgment (by even a small amount) can have a substantial effect.

The above results illustrate the kind of information that can be obtained. In order to more fully examine the consequences of using fallible judgment over a wide range of values of ϕ and br, tables were generated for all combinations of ϕ and br, using values of .1, .2, ..., .9 for each factor (81 combinations).[4] In all tables it was assumed that N_t = 1,000,000. Presentation of such a mass of data would be cumbersome at best. However, in order to get an idea of the results, data are presented for three conditions: (a) br = ϕ (for br = .40); (b) br = .50, ϕ = .10; and (c) br = .20, ϕ = .70. These specific values for br and ϕ were chosen since they illustrate a wide range of values for br and ϕ as well as show the effects when br and ϕ are similar as well as widely disparate.

Table 2 shows the results for situation (a). Not much commentary is necessary concerning Table 2 except to note that the largest decrease in percent errors occurs when ρ_{xy} increases from .9 to 1.0. Tables 3 and 4 show the results for situations (b) and (c) respectively.

Table 3 shows the results that occur when ϕ is considerably lower than the base rate. It is of interest to note the flatness of the relationship between ρ_{xy} and percent errors, as well as ρ_{xy} and nh (probability of a correct rejection). Furthermore, the N_a/N_r ratio gets quite small as ρ_{xy} increases. The reader is invited to examine Table 4 where ϕ is much larger than the base rate.

What are the implications that follow from these results? Although the results presented here are for a wide range of values of ρ_{xy} (assuming that ρ_{xy} is not negative--after appropriate rescaling), the research on clinical judgment has shown that the validity of judgments and criteria is low (e.g., Goldberg, 1965) or even zero (Einhorn, 1972). Therefore, the range of validities that are likely

Table 2

Error Indices as a Function of Judgment Fallibility:

$N_t = 1,000,000;\ br = .40 = \phi$

(1) ρ_{xy}	(2) N_a	(3) ph	(4) N_r	(5) nh	(6) N_a/N_r	(7) % errors	(8) $p(A\vert y \geq y_c)$	(9) $p(A\vert y < y_c)$
.00	240,000	.40	240,000	.60	1.0	48.0	.40	.40
.10	224,800	.44	224,800	.63	1.0	44.9	.44	.37
.20	209,600	.48	209,600	.65	1.0	41.9	.48	.35
.30	194,000	.52	194,000	.68	1.0	38.8	.52	.32
.40	178,000	.56	178,000	.70	1.0	35.6	.56	.30
.50	160,800	.60	160,800	.73	1.0	32.2	.60	.27
.60	142,400	.64	142,400	.76	1.0	28.5	.64	.24
.70	122,400	.69	122,400	.80	1.0	24.5	.69	.20
.80	98,800	.75	98,800	.84	1.0	19.8	.75	.16
.90	69,200	.83	69,200	.88	1.0	13.8	.83	.12
1.00	0	1.00	0	1.00	---	00.0	1.00	.00

Table 3

Error Indices as a Function of Judgment Fallibility:

$N_t = 1,000,000$; $br = .50$; $\phi = .10$

(1) ρ_{xy}	(2) N_a	(3) ph	(4) N_r	(5) nh	(6) N_a/N_r	(7) % Errors	(8) $p(A\|y \geq y_c)$	(9) $p(A\|y < y_c)$
.00	50,000	.50	450,000	.50	.11	50.0	.10	.10
.10	43,000	.57	443,000	.51	.10	48.6	.11	.09
.20	36,100	.64	436,100	.52	.08	47.2	.13	.07
.30	29,300	.71	429,300	.52	.07	45.8	.14	.06
.40	22,600	.77	422,600	.53	.05	44.5	.16	.05
.50	16,300	.84	416,300	.54	.04	43.2	.17	.03
.60	10,400	.90	410,400	.54	.03	42.1	.18	.02
.70	5,400	.95	405,400	.55	.01	41.0	.19	.01
.80	1,700	.98	401,700	.55	.004	40.3	.20	.003
.90	200	.998	400,200	.56	.0005	40.0	.20	.0004
1.00	0	1.00	400,000	.56	---	40.0	.20	.00

Table 4

Error Indices as a Function of Judgment Fallibility:

$N_t = 1,000,000$; br = .20; ϕ = .70

(1) ρ_{xy}	(2) N_a	(3) ph	(4) N_r	(5) nh	(6) N_a/N_r	(7) % Errors	(8) $p(A|y \geq y_c)$	(9) $p(A|y < y_c)$
.00	560,000	.20	60,000	.80	9.33	62.0	.70	.70
.10	550,900	.21	50,900	.83	10.82	60.2	.75	.69
.20	541,800	.23	41,800	.86	12.96	58.4	.79	.68
.30	532,700	.24	32,700	.89	16.29	56.5	.84	.67
.40	525,000	.25	25,000	.92	21.00	55.0	.88	.66
.50	517,300	.26	17,300	.94	29.90	53.5	.91	.65
.60	510,300	.27	10,300	.97	49.54	52.1	.95	.64
.70	505,400	.28	5,400	.98	93.59	51.1	.97	.63
.80	501,200	.28	1,200	.99	417.66	50.2	.99	.63
.90	500,500	.29	500	.99	1,000.95	50.1	.998	.63
1.00	500,000	.29	0	1.00	--	50.0	1.00	.625

to be encountered in actual tasks is truncated at the high
end. Moreover, in situations like welfare decisions, where
people being evaluated have a vested interest in being accepted, "game" aspects of the situation might make the validity of judgment even lower; i.e., people may give false
information to make themselves appear more "deserving." Giv-
en the substantial fallibility of judgment, the implication
is that large numbers of errors will be made. However, what
is more disturbing is that even if ρ_{xy} were quite high,
substantial numbers of errors will still be made. For example, consider Table 1 again and examine the results for
ρ_{xy} = .80. Even with such a high correlation, the percent
of errors is 18 percent. This error rate is even more disturbing since the error rate when ρ_{xy} = 0 is 38 percent.
(Another way to look at this is that an increase of 64 percent in explained variance results in only a 20 percent reduction in the number of errors.) For many combinations of
ϕ and br, large decreases in the number of errors do not
occur until ρ_{xy} is .9 or higher. One might argue that it
is unreasonable to expect human judgment to be as valid as
.9. The implication then is that we should lower our level
of aspiration with respect to the performance of administrators (and programs) to take into account man's cognitive
limitations (Simon, 1955; Dawes, 1976).

This last point raises several difficult issues. For
example, how is one to evaluate decision performance; i.e.,
at what level of ρ_{xy} is one willing to say that the decision maker is doing a good as opposed to a poor job. Related
to this is the problem of legal liability. At what level of
ρ_{xy} is someone "incompetent" and liable for damages? Is it
reasonable, for example, to expect medical doctors to have
validities greater than .9 (although even here errors will
be made)? If N_t is small, is it "worth it" to try to improve judgmental validity since the decrease in number of
errors (as well as % errors) is likely to be small? While I
have no answers to these questions, whatever answers evolve
will obviously have important policy implications.

The second set of implications to be drawn from these
results concerns the setting of ϕ. If one assumes that the
fallibility of judgment remains constant for different values of ϕ, then the setting of ϕ is a major determinant
of the trade-off between the two types of errors. A good
way to see this is to examine Figure 1 and imagine that x_c
is moved either to the left or right. In either case, the
reduction of one type of error must <u>increase</u> the other type
of error. For example, consider that the judgment of need
and "true need" in the welfare situation was as high as
ρ_{xy} = .70. Table 5 shows the results that would occur if

Table 5

Errors for Two Levels of the Selection Ratio:

$$N_t = 1,000,000; \; br = .30; \; \rho_{xy} = .70$$

$\phi = .20$	$\phi = .40$
$N_a = 56,000$	$N_a = 172,000$
$N_r = 156,000$	$N_r = 72,000$
$N_a/N_r = .36$	$N_a/N_r = 2.39$
% errors = 21.1%	% errors = 24.4%

the values used in Table 1 were used, i.e., br = .30, ϕ = .20, N_t = 1,000,000. Now suppose that certain welfare officials react with horror at the trade-off of .36 since it means that for every cheater there are 2.79 people who are being cheated out of welfare. Suppose that armed with these facts, the administrators get more money so that ϕ can be raised to .40 (from .20). The results of raising ϕ to .40 are shown in the second column of Table 5. By increasing ϕ, the N_a/N_r ratio is almost reversed; the number of people cheated out of welfare, N_r, is reduced from 156,000 to 72,000 (a reduction of 54 percent) <u>at the cost of</u> increasing the number of welfare cheats from 56,000 to 172,000 (a 307% increase). Furthermore, note that the percent errors also increases from 21.2 percent to 24.4 percent. Is such a change in policy "worth it"? Reasonable people with differing value systems will undoubtedly disagree about this. However, while one's values are implicit in any decision that is made, both administrators and the public are entitled to know what these implicit trade-offs are so that discussion can take place as to what they should be.

A more general point can be made with respect to ϕ. When ϕ is low, this protects against making large numbers of acceptance errors (at the cost of greater rejection errors--see Table 3). In effect, low ϕ means that the cost of acceptance errors outweighs the cost of rejection errors. Of course, the reverse is true if ϕ is large. The latter case leads to an interesting attribution. Consider that surgeons feel that rejection errors (i.e., not operating on someone who needs the surgery) are much more costly than acceptance errors (unnecessary surgery). Therefore, they set ϕ high. Given the fallibility of judgment, there will be a very large number of unnecessary surgeries. This result may be attributed to the "greed" of surgeons although an alternative explanation points to the fallibility of judgment combined with the perceived relative costs of errors.

While many factors can influence the setting of ϕ, very little systematic research has been done to isolate what these are. One factor may be the ability to reverse one's decision after realizing it was a mistake. For example, university tenure decisions are basically irreversible. This may cause ϕ to be set low since an acceptance error cannot be corrected. A second factor may be the ease with which the costs of the two types of errors can be calculated. For example, acceptance errors can usually be calculated in terms of dollars (e.g., typical headline, "Welfare cheating costs state $X million a year"), while the cost of rejection errors is harder to calculate. In cases like this, trapped administrators may be adept at setting ϕ so that N_a is small, although N_r may be quite large. If ρ_{xy} were low/ moderate (as all the research shows), small N_a will usually mean that N_r is large. Therefore, in a paradoxical way, welfare cheating, unnecessary surgery, etc., may be necessary! A third factor that can affect ϕ is the total number of applicants, N_t. This can occur if the total number of accepts (N) is fixed (usually because of budget constraints). Since,

$$N = N_t \phi \quad , \tag{11}$$

increases in N_t must result in lowered ϕ in order to keep N a constant. If the political strategy is to keep N a constant (or reduce it), increases in N_t, followed by decreases in ϕ, must imply a change in the trade-off relationship between the types of errors that will be made.

Finally, it should be pointed out that the setting of ϕ in actual settings may be done without explicit consideration of the base rate and/or the fallibility of judgment (for example, administrators may try to maximize their budgets for political reasons, leading to $\phi > br$). The present results clearly show that both br and ρ_{xy} are important in setting ϕ vis-a-vis the kinds of errors that will occur.

Individual vs. Societal Decisions

The analysis thus far has been concerned with errors that result from the use of fallible judgment as viewed by the decision maker. Another side of the question concerns the effect that fallible judgment has from the individual's perspective. For example, if someone were truly in need of welfare, what is the probability of being accepted to get it, as a function of the fallibility of judgment? A reasonable way of answering this question is to determine the probability of being accepted given $y \geq y_c$, i.e.:

$$p(x \geq x_c | y \geq y_c) = \frac{p(y \geq y_c | x \geq x_c) p(x \geq x_c)}{p(y \geq y_c)}$$

$$p(A | y \geq y_c) = \frac{p h(\phi)}{br} \quad . \tag{12}$$

Similarly, one can determine the probability of being accepted given that $y < y_c$, i.e.,

$$p(A | y < y_c) = p(x \geq x_c | y < y_c) = \frac{f p(\phi)}{1 - br} \quad . \tag{13}$$

Equations (12) and (13) are easily computed for values of

ρ_{xy}, ϕ, and br (under the assumptions made earlier). As a matter of fact, columns (8) and (9) in all of the previous tables show these probabilities as a function of ρ_{xy}. In order to illustrate, consider Table 1 again. Note that $p(A|y \geq y_c)$ increases very slowly as a function of ρ_{xy}. Moreover, the improvement in the probability over chance ($\rho_{xy} = 0$) is remarkably small--in fact, even if $\rho_{xy} = .70$, the person who deserves the acceptance has less than a .5 chance of getting it. On the other hand, the probability of receiving A given $y < y_c$ is not reduced greatly until ρ_{xy} gets quite high. Therefore, for an individual, being above y_c does not mean that acceptance is assured, <u>even if</u> judgment is quite highly valid. Furthermore, when ρ_{xy} is low/moderate, the probability of getting A when $y < y_c$ is substantial.

The earlier discussion of the effect of ϕ is particularly pertinent to understanding the behavior of (12) and (13). When ϕ is low, the probability of being accepted, given $y \geq y_c$, does not dramatically increase with increases in ρ_{xy} (especially in the range that ρ_{xy} takes in practice). The implications for individuals who apply in low ϕ situations is that even if judgment is highly valid, and if they are particularly deserving, the probability of acceptance may not be very high. As an example, consider Table 3 again. Column (8) shows the extreme insensitivity of this probability to the fallibility of judgment. Moreover, note that column (9) shows that even with an extremely low ϕ, if ρ_{xy} is low undeserving people will still get accepted. Table 4 shows what happens when ϕ is large--the probability of being accepted is high regardless of one's position on the criterion (one implication of this is that hypochondria can be harmful to your health).

Base Rates

The concept of base rates is clearly of great importance in decision making (cf. Meehl & Rosen, 1955). As the above analysis indicates, the base rate enters prominently in the various error indices. However, there are several troubling aspects about this. The first has to do with the accumulating evidence that people ignore base rate information even when it is given to them in explicit form (Tversky & Kahneman, 1974; Lyon & Slovic, 1976; Nisbett et al., 1976). One reason advanced for this is given by Nisbett et al. (1976): "Almost by its very nature, base-rate or consensus information is remote, pallid, and abstract. In contrast, target case information is vivid, salient, and concrete" (p. 128). If base rate information is ignored in studies where it can be easily obtained, the problems of

Table 6

Error Indices for Two Time Periods:

$\phi = .50;\ \rho_{xy} = .40$

	N_t	N	br	N_a	N_r	$N_a + N_r$	N_a/N_r	% Errors	$p(A|y \geq y_c)$	$p(A|y < y_c)$
t_1	1,000,000	500,000	.60	137,000	237,000	374,000	.58	37.4	.61	.34
t_2	1,200,000	600,000	.54	192,000	240,000	432,000	.80	36.0	.63	.35

using base rates in natural situations are compounded because
it is not easy to know what they are. For example, what is
the base rate of "true need" for welfare? Clearly, the first
problem is to define the population that one is interested in.
Therefore, estimating base rates means that careful consideration must be given to defining the population of interest.

Let us say that the decision maker is convinced of the
importance of estimating base rates. However, since the base
rate is a probability, might not the heuristics that are used
for making probability judgments distort these estimated values? It seems likely that the base rate would be particularly vulnerable to the "availability" heuristic; i.e., judgment
of probability is determined by the ease with which relevant
instances are imagined or can be retrieved from memory. The
role of the mass media in particular can significantly alter
the perception of base rates (cf. Slovic, Fischhoff, & Lichtenstein, 1976). If policy makers' perceptions of base rates
are influenced by availability heuristics, and ϕ is then
set with respect to these estimated base rates, various unin-
tended consequences can occur. For example, let us say that
a policy maker wishes to set $N_a/N_r = 1$. However, due to a
great deal of publicity, etc., he estimates the base rate at
a value higher than it actually is. Therefore, by setting
ϕ to an inflated value of the base rate, the consequence is
to make more N_a than N_r. This example is not intended to
discourage explicit consideration of the base rate--quite the
contrary. It does illustrate that care should be exercised
in making probability judgments, including base rates (see
Hogarth, 1975). In actual practice, decision makers would be
wise to consider sensitivity analyses of the various error
indices with respect to estimates of the base rate.

Feedback Effects

When dealing with decision making in complex social systems, various mechanisms may not be evident before actual implementation of any program. One extremely important factor
that is often overlooked is the feedback effect that the outcomes of decisions at one time can have on behavior at a later time. While this topic needs much more careful study, an
example will be used to illustrate the effect. Consider that
a program is set up to alleviate some poverty related problem.
Furthermore, for the sake of discussion, assume that at the
end of the first year of operation, $N_t = 1,000,000$; $br =
.60$; $\phi = .50$; and $\rho_{xy} = .40$. Table 6 shows the various er-
ror values that would result. The important thing to note is
that $p(A|y < y_c)$ is quite high. One could hypothesize that
the ease of being accepted given $y < y_c$ would become widely
known (e.g., the "word" gets out that it's easy to qualify

for the program). The effect of such information could be an increase in the number of undeserving (i.e., $y < y_c$) people applying in the next time period. Let us assume that in the second time period, 200,000 more people apply than in time 1 (i.e., $N_t = 1,200,000$) but that 150,000 of these are $y < y_c$ and 50,000 are $y \geq y_c$. If ρ_{xy} remains at .40 (it might drop due to the increased work load) and ϕ is not changed, the number and kinds of errors that result are shown in the second row of Table 6. Note that N_a increases considerably while N_r also increases. The number of total errors is increased from 374,000 to 432,000 (a difference of 58,000) at the added cost of 100,000 extra acceptances. Therefore, although more people are being accepted (and the program is more costly to run), N_r is not reduced and N_a is considerably increased. One very disturbing aspect of this scenario is that the cost of maintaining this program increases as the number of both types of errors increases.

Of crucial concern to policy makers (and tax payers) is the fate of programs over longer time periods. One possibility is that such programs will continue to deteriorate (i.e., more errors and more money to support them) until the whole system must be abandoned. A second possibility is that the system will stabilize at some point in time. Whether one outcome or the other will occur should depend (in part) on the degree to which information about the system is transmitted to the $y < y_c$ and $y \geq y_c$ groups and their respective reactions to this information. Clearly, more research is needed on the diffusion of information process and the factors that influence behavioral reactions to this information. Although the example given here is admittedly contrived, it does illustrate the strong effects that feedback can have.[5]

Regression Effects

What causes these results? The answer concerns "regression effects" in conjunction with values of br and ϕ. Since judgment is fallible, criterion scores must be regressive with respect to judgment (and vice versa--cf. Einhorn and Schacht, 1977). As Kahneman and Tversky (1973) point out:

> Regression effects are all about us. In our experience, most outstanding fathers have somewhat disappointing sons, brilliant wives have duller husbands, the ill-adjusted tend to adjust and the fortunate are eventually stricken by ill luck. In spite of these encounters, people do not acquire a proper notion of regression. First, they do not expect regression in many situations where it is bound to occur. Second, as any teacher of

statistics will attest, a proper notion of regression is extremely difficult to acquire. Third, when people observe regression, they typically invent spurious dynamic explanations for it. (pp. 249-50)

Even those who have studied statistics are surprised by the power of regression effects. For example, consider that you judge someone to be $x = 3.0$, i.e., three standard deviations above the mean. Furthermore, let us assume that your judgment is highly valid, $\rho_{xy} = .80$. What is the probability that the true/criterion score will be at least three standard deviations above the mean? The answer is .16.[6] A disturbing aspect of this result is that people seem to have most confidence in extreme judgments although these are the ones that will be most regressive (Kahneman & Tversky, 1973).

Another way to look at regression effects is from a Bayesian perspective. This has the advantage of showing the relationship between the fallibility of judgment and both the base rate and selection ratio. If one is interested in predicting y from x, the base rate is the prior probability of a "success"; i.e., it is unconditional on specific evidence. In order to update the prior probability on the basis of specific evidence (in this case, the judgment x), one needs the diagnosticity of the evidence (called the "likelihood"). In a rough way, ρ_{xy} tells us the diagnostic value of any x. Therefore, the specific values (or range of values) of x, and ρ_{xy}, are combined with the prior to yield a posterior probability. However, regression effects occur because as soon as $\rho_{xy} \neq 1.0$, the diagnosticity of the data drops precipitously. Therefore, when the prior is either high or low, judgment should (in a normative statistical sense) have little effect. For example, in the problem in the preceding paragraph, the prior probability, $p(y \geq 3)$, is only .001. Therefore, even with $x = 3$ and $\rho_{xy} = .8$, the posterior probability, $p(y \geq 3 | x = 3, \rho_{xy} = .8) = .16$, is still low (although higher than the prior). Therefore, although valid judgment changes the prior probability, these changes tend to be much less than we intuitively expect.

The same logic holds if one is interested in predicting x from y; for example, given that one is very deserving ($y = 2$), how likely is it that one will be judged as sufficiently deserving to be accepted ($x \geq x_c$)? In this case, the prior probability is equivalent to ϕ, the selection ratio. The given information is now y, and ρ_{xy} again reflects diagnosticity. To illustrate, consider that a certain journal only accepts 10 percent of the manuscripts submitted to it ($\phi = .10$). You write a truly outstanding paper ($y = 2.0$) and submit it. If the validity of reviewers' judgments were

ρ_{xy} = 70, what is the probability of having the article ac-
cepted? The answer is .58, i.e., $p(x \geq 1.25 | y = 2, \rho_{xy} =$
.7) = .58. Therefore, if your paper is truly exceptional <u>and</u>
judgment is highly valid, the chance of acceptance is just
over one half.

Assumptions

The present analysis is based on the assumptions that x
and y are standardized and that x and y follow a bivariate normal distribution (which implies a linear relationship
between judgment and criterion). (These assumptions are discussed in greater detail in Einhorn and Schacht (1977).) The
former assumption means that one must be careful to specify
the population that one is standardizing against. This population should be defined vis-a-vis those "applying" as opposed to the general population. The second assumption may
not hold for all situations (indeed, this is a topic for further study). However, although the specific values presented
here might change under different assumptions regarding the
joint and marginal distributions of x and y, the basic
principles discussed here are unaffected. Therefore, the dilemmas that fallible judgment poses for social policy remain.

Conclusion

The fact that judgment is fallible is obvious; the implications of fallibility for social policy are not. This
paper has tried to explore some of these implications by focusing on the variables that are implicit in the decision
making process. By making these factors explicit, it is
hoped that some of the basic issues have been clarified and a
framework for further study has been established. Such study
should concern both practical questions (e.g., How does one
determine ρ_{xy}, ϕ, and br in any given situation?) as
well as conceptual issues (e.g., How does one judge the
trade-off between errors? What is "incompetence"? Under
what conditions will social programs work or fail? How can
one increase ρ_{xy} and is it "worth it"? Is the cost of
maintaining a bureaucracy worth whatever increase in ρ_{xy}
one might get over random selection?). Let us hope that social science can rise to these challenges.

References

Campbell, D. T. Reforms as experiments. <u>American Psycholo-
gist</u>, 1969, <u>24</u>, 409-429.

Cronbach, L. J., & Gleser, G. C. <u>Psychological tests and
personnel decisions</u> (2nd edition). Urbana, Ill.:
University of Illinois Press, 1965.

Dawes, R. M.   Shallow psychology.   In J. Carroll and J. Payne
    (Eds.), Cognition and social behavior.   Hillsdale, New
    Jersey: Lawrence Erlbaum, 1976.

Edwards, W.   Conservatism in human information processing.
    In B. Kleinmuntz (Eds.), Formal representation of human
    judgment.   New York: Wiley, 1968.

Einhorn, H. J.   Expert measurement and mechanical combination.
    Organizational Behavior and Human Performance, 1972, 7,
    86-106.

Einhorn, H. J., & Schacht, S.   Decisions based on fallible
    clinical judgment.   In M. Kaplan & S. Schwartz (Eds.),
    Judgment and decision processes in applied settings.
    New York: Academic Press, 1977.

Elstein, A. S.   Clinical judgment: Psychological research
    and medical practice.   Science, 1976, 194, 696-700.

Goldberg, L. R.   Diagnosticians vs. diagnostic signs: The
    diagnosis of psychosis vs. neurosis from the M.M.P.I.
    Psychological Monographs, 1965, 79, No. 602.

Hammond, K. R., & Adelman, L.   Science, values, and human
    judgment.   Science, 1976, 194, 389-396.

Hogarth, R. M.   Cognitive processes and the assessment of
    subjective probability distributions.   Journal of the
    American Statistical Association, 1975, 70, 271-294.

Kahneman, D., & Tversky, A.   On the psychology of prediction.
    Psychological Review, 1973, 80, 237-251.

Lyon, D., & Slovic, P.   Dominance of accuracy information and
    neglect of base rates in probability estimation.   Acta
    Psychologica, 1976, 40, 287-298.

Meehl, P. E., & Rosen, A.   Antecedent probability and the
    efficiency of psychometric signs, patterns, or cutting
    scores.   Psychological Bulletin, 1955, 52, 194-216.

Nisbett, R. E., Borgida, E., Crandall, R., & Reed, H.   Popu-
    lar induction: Information is not necessarily informa-
    tive.   In J. Carroll & J. Payne (Eds.), Cognition and
    social behavior.   Hillsdale, New Jersey: Lawrence Erl-
    baum, 1976.

Pearson, K. Tables for statisticians and biometricians.
    London: University College, 1931.

Simon, H. A behavioral model of rational choice. Quarterly
    Journal of Economics, 1955, 69, 99-118.

Slovic, P. From Shakespeare to Simon: Speculations--and
    some evidence--about man's ability to process informa-
    tion. Oregon Research Institute Monograph, 1974, 12, 2.

Slovic, P., & McPhillamy, D. Dimensional commensurability
    and cue utilization in comparative judgment. Organiza-
    tional Behavior and Human Performance, 1974, 11, 172-194.

Slovic, P., Fischhoff, B., & Lichtenstein, S. Cognitive pro-
    cesses and societal risk taking. In J. Carroll and J.
    Payne (Eds.), Cognition and social behavior. Hillsdale,
    New Jersey: Lawrence Erlbaum, 1976.

Taylor, H. C., & Russell, J. T. The relationship of validity
    coefficients to the practical effectiveness of tests in
    selection: Discussion and tables. Journal of Applied
    Psychology, 1939, 23, 565-578.

Tversky, A., & Kahneman, D. Judgment under uncertainty:
    Heuristics and biases. Science, 1974, 185, 1124-1131.

Footnotes

I would like to thank the following people for their
comments on an earlier draft of this paper: Ken Hammond,
Paul Hirsch, Robin Hogarth, Howard Kunreuther, and John
Payne. Special thanks are due to Don Kleinmuntz for his
programming help.

[1] Since any decision implies differential actions, one
might argue that treatment effects must always be confounded
with judgmental accuracy. However, at least a quantitative
difference exists between situations where the "accept" decision is then followed by some treatment specifically aimed
at changing y (remedial reading, for example) and those
where the accept/reject decision is not followed by specific
attempts to change y (e.g., welfare).

[2] Note that the error probabilities (false positive and
false negative rates) are not defined as Type I and II errors, since they are conditional on the judgment and not the
true score.

[3]Let, $f(x, y)$ = bivariate normal distribution; $ph = p(y \geq y_c | x \geq x_c) = p(y \geq y_c \cap x \geq x_c) p(x \geq x_c)$. However:

$$p(y \geq y_c \cap x \geq x_c) = \int_{x_c}^{\infty} \int_{y_c}^{\infty} f(x, y) \, dx \, dy \, .$$

x_c is the point on the marginal distribution of x such that, $1 - F(x_c) = \phi$, where, F = cumulative normal distribution.

y_c is the point on the marginal distribution of y such that, $1 - F(y_c) = br$.

Tables of the joint probabilities are available (Pearson, 1931). Tables for positive hit rates for values of ρ_{xy} ϕ, and br are also available (Taylor & Russell, 1939).

[4]A computer program has been developed which will print out tables like those shown here. The input necessary is simply N_t, br, and ϕ. A listing is available from the author.

[5]Another factor that may influence the degree to which social programs iterate to stability or chaos has been pointed out to me by Kurt Snapper. If someone qualifies for a particular program, this may be taken as evidence that they are eligible to receive other programs. Therefore, an original mistake may have greater consequences than for just one program.

[6]In general, one can determine the probability that $y \geq \alpha$ (for any α in standard scores) given ρ_{xy} and x, i.e., $p(y \geq \alpha | x, \rho_{xy})$. Note that $\hat{y} = \rho_{xy} x$ (from regression theory). Furthermore, $E(y|x) = \hat{y}$ and the standard deviation in any array is given by $(1 - \rho_{xy}^2)^{1/2}$. Therefore:

$$p(y \geq \alpha | x, \rho_{xy}) = 1 - F\left[\frac{\alpha - \hat{y}}{(1 - \rho_{xy}^2)^{1/2}} \right]$$

where F = cumulative normal distribution. In the example, $\alpha = x = 3.0$, and $\rho_{xy} = .8$. Since x is also regressive with respect to y, a similar argument holds for determining $p(x \geq \alpha | y, \rho_{xy})$.

Further Reading

S.R. Arnstein and A.N. Christakis, <u>Perspectives on Technology Assessment</u> (Crofton Publishing Corp., Newton, Mass., 1975).

R.V. Brown, A.S. Kahar and C. Peterson, <u>Decision Analysis for the Manager</u> (Holt, Rinehart and Winston, NY, 1974).

J.S. Carroll and J.W. Payne (Eds.), <u>Cognition and Social Behavior</u> (Erlbaum, Hillsdale, NY, 1976).

I.L. Horwitz (Ed.), <u>The Use and Abuse of Social Science: Behavioral Research and Policy Making, 2nd Edition</u> (Transaction Books, New Brunswick, 1975).

M.F. Kaplan and S. Schwartz (Eds.), <u>Human Judgment and Decision Processes: Applications in Problem Settings</u> (Academic Press, NY, 1977).

R.L. Keeney and H. Raiffa, <u>Decision with Multiple Objectives: Preferences and Value Tradeoffs</u> (John Wiley and Sons, NY, 1976).

P. Slovic, B. Fischhoff and S. Lichtenstein, "Behavioral Decision Theory" in <u>Annual Review of Psychology</u>, 1977, <u>28</u>: 1-39.

L.A. Zadeh, K. Fu, K. Tanaka and M. Shimura (Eds.) <u>Fuzzy Sets and Their Applications to Cognitive and Decision Processes</u> (Academic Press, NY, 1975).

Journals

Policy Sciences
Management Science
Technology Forecasting and Social Change
Futures
Operations Research
Socioeconomic Planning Sciences
Organizational Behavior and Human Performance

Index

academic community, 58
accuracy, 146
agenda, 112
aggregation functions, 17
ammunition, 128
analytical experimentation, 15
assessment, 113
  risk, 98
associations, producer, 9
attitude, 86
availability bias, 100

bananas, 9
base rates, 161
bauxite, 8
Bayes, 165
  theorem, 73, 75
beliefs, perseverance of, 102
biases, 102
body politic, 36
  See also Government
bullet, 128
bureaucracy, 55

cartels, 8
clinical inference, 18
clinical trials, 19
coefficient, valuation, 112
coffee, 8
conflict, 17, 38, 44, 59, 70, 91
conformity, 115

control, 13
  groups, 19
coordination, 114
copper, 8
correlation, 90
court, science, 124
covertness, 15
criterion, 145

decision, 2, 3, 17, 55, 84, 91, 112, 113, 115, 160
  errors, 143
  public policy, 6
  theory, 143
decision-maker, 119
  political, 2
decision-making, 24, 43, 44, 72, 99
disentanglement, 16

economists, 112
economy, 6
efficacy-1, definition of, 74
efficacy-2, definition of, 74
efficacy-3, 74
error, 26, 144, 163
estimation, 26
ethics, 115
evaluation, 89, 112
experimentation, 15, 19
expert, definition of, 57